Northwestern University

STUDIES IN *Phenomenology &*

Existential Philosophy

Speaking
(La Parole)

Georges Gusdorf

Translated, with an introduction by

SPEAKING
(La Parole)

PAUL T. BROCKELMAN

NORTHWESTERN UNIVERSITY PRESS

1 9 6 5

La Parole was published by Presses Universitaires de France, Paris, in 1953.

Translation copyright © 1965 by Paul T. Brockelman
Library of Congress Catalog Card Number: 65-14811
Printed in the United States of America
ISBN 0-8101-0111-4
Second printing, 1970

Acknowledgements for the
English Edition

I WISH TO THANK Presses Universitaires de France for permission to translate and publish this work by Professor Gusdorf. I am indebted to Mr. Edouard Morot-Sir, the Cultural Adviser of the French Embassy in this country and the Representative for the French Universities in the United States, for information concerning the life and career of M. Gusdorf. Further, I wish to express my thanks to Professors John Wild and James Edie for their helpful advice concerning the preparation of this manuscript. Thanks must likewise be extended to my colleagues, Professors Asher Moore and Peter Sylvester, for reading the manuscript and making several helpful suggestions. I am indebted to my wife for her help in matters of style and expression as well as her constant rereading of the text. I am especially indebted to Prof. David Mitchell of the University of Chicago, who spent many long hours going over the text with me. Finally, I wish to thank the Graduate School of the University of New Hampshire for a research grant to help in the preparation of this book.

P. T. B.

Introduction

ANOTHER PHILOSOPHY of language? Is it possible? Will we not drown in analyses of language? After all, the philosophy of language, whether in the form of Logical Atomism, Logical Positivism, or Linguistic and Conceptual Analysis, has dominated the English-speaking philosophic scene for almost fifty years. Although this little book represents a different tradition, is it not analogous to an attempt by an Englishman to teach the French how to cook, Persians how to make rugs, Russians how to dance, or Americans how to sell soap?

Perhaps. We all know of the apparent gulf that divides contemporary philosophy into two camps: Anglo-Saxon philosophy with its present focus on conceptual analysis or ordinary language philosophy, centered at Oxford; and continental philosophy with its focus on existential phenomenology, centered in France and Germany. But as several writers have recently noted, such mutual antagonism and misunderstanding need not be the case, for the two traditions overlap in many of their typical concerns and themes. I do not mean to imply, of course, that with a bit of open-mindedness the two sides would in fact discover that they are doing and saying the same thing. Hardly. Nevertheless, it is still true that they are closer than might be at first imagined, closer for instance than a Russell or a Moore is to a Bosanquet or a Bradley. Both traditions fundamentally hark back to a rejection of idealism. Both attempt to turn to the concrete as opposed to abstraction, one in the form of "common sense" and the other in the form of "concrete reality." Both are suspicious of abstraction and the attempt to deduce knowledge from speculative premises. In fact, both are suspicious of speculative metaphysics *per se*. Neither holds systems in high esteem, preferring a piecemeal but rigorous analysis of a given concept or phenomenon. And all phenomenologists, whether of the "pure" or "existential" variety, would unhesitatingly go along with that famous dictum of Wittgenstein: "Look, don't think!" Insofar, then, as both hold to a kind of empiricism that insists, ultimately, on referring all concepts to concrete experience, they are allies. In fact, taking the name from William James, existential phenomenology has sometimes been referred to as "radical empiricism."

But these rather general similarities are relatively unimportant. Of far more importance is the convergence of these two traditions with respect to the philosophy of language. First of all, language has come to be a central concern for both. For example, Heidegger, in his later writings, has come to dwell extensively upon language. And Maurice Merleau-Ponty, the central figure in contemporary French phenomenology, came more and more until his untimely death to treat expression (and language as a form of expression) as fundamentally and crucially important to human reality.

These two traditions likewise concur on the importance of "ordinary language" as opposed to "ideal" languages. For both, "ideal" languages presuppose and assume ordinary usage and can never presume to replace that ordinary usage. Meaning does not exist in an ideal realm of perfect clarity and distinctness, apart from and antedating the ambiguous domain of ordinary usage. To clear up ordinary language may be pragmatically valuable, but it is at the same time reductive. Meaning emerges in ordinary usage and always presupposes it. Ordinary languages are not so many slipshod and inferior inventions to express ideal meanings. Further, both would agree, no word has a single meaning as its essence. Words have many meanings, depending upon the context of their usage. To talk of the existence of God, for example, is not at all the same thing as to talk of the existence of this book. The meaning of words and concepts cannot be grasped in isolation, but only within the context of their usage, or within the horizon of the situation in which they are expressed. In phenomenological terms, words are "expressions" or perspectives upon intended meanings. We see meaning through words, and therefore words carry different meanings in different contexts.

And insofar as the Oxford analysts wish to imply by "ordinary language" a concrete and multi-dimensional reality as the ultimate context of the emergence of meaning, and against the background of which the technical or ideal languages emerge and make sense, then, I think that they are in closer agreement with the continental philosophers than either might think. The phenomenological conception of *Lebenswelt* or *être au monde* is meant to express a similar concrete reality, a similar chrysalis of meaning, and a similar background

from which science and religion, for instance, emerge
and make sense. Both of these endeavors, after all, are
meaningful, if at all, *for* human beings and *within*
human experience and history. A Scientific or religious
universe makes sense only as a "sub-universe" of the
lived world, only as a project, toward objective understanding or personal salvation, of living, experiencing,
bodily persons.[1] As one philosopher has put it: "Ordinary language is to the technical languages as the
Lebenswelt is to the sciences." [2]

This is, of course, only a brief and general indication
of some of the similarities shared by the two traditions.
It is by no means true that the insights of both converge
on all points, or even most. In fact, they do not. But there
may be enough similar interests and views to allow for
dialogue. Although this book represents only an introduction to a phenomenology of language, and an introduction meant for the general French public at that, it is
still hoped that it will prove interesting and rewarding
for English and American readers, both on its merits as
an introductory piece of existential phenomenology as
well as a contribution from that camp to the philosophy
of language in general.

What, then, the reader might ask, are some of the

1. The endeavor to leave existence alone, to not translate it
into idea, is a desire apparently shared by Wittgenstein. "Kierkegaard and Wittgenstein find the world suffering from illusions,
and write to free us of them." Stanley Cavell, "Existentialism
and Analytical Philosophy," *Daedalus*, Summer 1964. As Kierkegaard wishes to free the reader to withdraw from the illusion
of living abstractly in order to be himself, Wittgenstein wants
merely to dissolve the problems, to release the fly from the bottle,
and to leave everything as it is.

2. For an interesting view concerning the relation of existen-
tial phenomenology and ordinary language philosophy, see John
Wild, "Is there a World of Ordinary Language?," *Philosophical
Review*, LXVII, 1958, pp. 460–76.

typical themes that characterize existential phenomenology in general and its philosophy of language in particular?

Generally, existential phenomenologists orient their reflections around two seminal notions—that of the primacy of existence as lived and the necessity of a "phenomenological" and purely descriptive analysis of such experience in order to noetically and verbally express it. It will not take very long for the reader to recognize this dual theme as the implicit background from which *Speaking* has emerged, and over against which it must be understood.

For any existing man, concrete experience or the lived texture of his subjective life is what he is initially given and what he lives from day to day. Whatever we come to know about the world in itself, others, eternal truths, etc., can be gained only through experience. As a subject, I am not first of all a certain "nature," nor a set of bodily mechanisms—rather I am a lived body experiencing myself, the world, the past, and others around me. If a man is sometimes an object to himself, to be observed as a member of a class and susceptible as a member of that class to general predications and universal characteristics, still, he is not *only* this, nor even primarily this. He is first of all a subject, a living, experiencing being. *As such,* he is never an object to himself, for his lived experience is never observable externally qua experience. The texture of experience is subjective or lived.

Since the experiencing process cannot be externally observed, neither can it be apprehended by means of the abstraction of common characteristics from several instances of it (I have direct access only to *my* existence as lived, and I do not observe it—I live it). Because of this, a new *method* of knowing, indeed a different *sense* of knowing, is called for, a method which can gain access to subjective experience as such and which at the same time will not reduce such experience to abstract and general truths—essences. The existential phenomenologists generally find this epistemic process in phenomenological description. The second general theme of this movement, then, is to be found in the attempt to describe reflectively the lived sense of various experiential phenomena as we live them, to make explicit that sense which is implicit to any kind of experience. The aim of such a descriptive analysis is neither to grasp a quidity or set of characteristics shared by members of a class, nor is it to conduct an empirical investigation of the factual material involved in any subjective phenomenon (e.g. my remembering my grandmother). Rather, it attempts to express the sense or meaning (*die Bedeutung,* Heidegger calls it) of any lived phenomenon as it is lived, in and through any particular case.

Thus, beginning with Heidegger, existential phenomenologists unite various themes from the earlier existential and phenomenological movements. On the one hand, the primacy of existence or concrete experience is assumed. On the other hand, the phenomenological method of descriptive analysis is taken over as the appropriate means of apprehending such experience. And lastly, besides the primacy of lived existence and the phenomenological method of description, existential phenomenologists (including Gusdorf) generally accept the conception of "world," i.e. the "intentionality" or correlativity of subject and object in experience. Experience as lived is a "field," and subject and object are integrated into that field as moments of it.

We are born into a horizon or "world" of correlative experiences. We *are* these experiences, dumbly lived first of all. But we can reflectively describe the lived sense of such experiential and worldly phenomena, and the body of such phenomenological descriptions constitutes existential phenomenology.

Now, since language and expression generally constitute one such central phenomenon of existence, and since this book is an attempt to introduce us to a descriptive analysis of speaking, let us see in a bit more detail how existential phenomenology treats such a topic, and in what sense such an analysis differs from traditional philosophical treatments of language.

It is of course a generalization, but perhaps a fair one in this instance, to divide the history of the philosophy of language into two primary traditions. On the one hand, we have such philosophers as Plato, Leibniz, and, apparently, the early Husserl, who espouse an idealism or rationalism of language. Words are simply vehicles, vehicles of ideal signification. Language is composed of signs that point the mind to ideal meanings—meanings which are the objects of true knowledge. In a certain sense, languages are the shabby means invented by the mind to communicate concepts. Thus, clearly, our task is to become conceptually clear. This will necessarily entail a clearing-up of ambiguous and slipshod ordinary language, a translation of language into its ideal essence. Language is mind in the act of communication.

On the other hand, we have the empiricist interpretation of language, such as that of Locke and Hume. Again, words refer to meanings outside themselves, to concepts. But now these concepts are not constitutive of reality as with the idealist. On the contrary, they are in fact merely products of the generalizing and synthetic capacities of the associating mind. Thus, word-signs stimulate the associating mind to refer to meanings or ideas lodged within itself and ultimately derived from the interaction of impressions and that associating mind. We find that "the meaning of words is considered to be given with the stimuli or with the states of consciousness which it is simply a matter of naming; the shape of the word, as heard or phonetically formed, is given with the cerebral or mental tracks; speech is not an action and does not show up the internal possibilities of the subject: man can speak as the electric lamp can become incandescent." [3]

We can note at least three assumptions common to these two traditions. First, language is discussed predominantly (at least until Romanticism) as a mode of thought. This is true for both traditions. Thought seemingly invents language in order to express itself. Both treat "language essentially in its theoretical content." [4] Secondly, both traditions assume that the meaning of words is detached from the signs that refer to it, residing either in a cognitive heaven of pure ideas or in the capacities of the associating mind to derive meaning from a welter of impressions. At any rate, for both, language is a collection of signs referring to ideas outside themselves.[5] Thirdly, these primary traditions obviously embody a radical dualism—for the one reduces language to an affair of the mind and the other to a state of the body. Now, as we shall see, a phenomenology of language

3. M. Merleau-Ponty, *Phenomenology of Perception,* New York, 1962, p. 175.

4. Ernst Cassirer, *The Philosophy of Symbolic Forms,* Vol. 1, New Haven, 1953, p. 147.

5. *Ibid.,* p. 148.

differs quite significantly from either of these approaches to language.

Husserl, in his earlier writings, treated languages as systems of signs that refer for their particular meaning to an ideal language grasped eidetically through the various ordinary languages. In later years, however, consonant with the movement of his phenomenological philosophy toward the conception of the *Lebenswelt* in his final work, Husserl treated language in terms of the speaking subject, and indicated that it was the substance of thought.[6] It is this direction, this turn toward the speaking subject, that existential phenomenology has developed since that time, and that can best be seen in Merleau-Ponty's phenomenology of language.

First of all, unlike the traditional approaches, Merleau-Ponty claims for his philosophy that it is non-dualistic. Each person is a being-in-the-world, a subjectively lived experience stretched out toward things and others. This is not a mental or spiritual phenomenon, but rather a bodily experience, a bodily insertion in the world. However, in this context, I am not a body-machine, for the body which Merleau-Ponty is talking about is the lived-body (*le corps vecu*)—the bodily experience of seeing, touching, hearing, loving, finding, losing, etc. I am *neither* a machine as observed externally, nor am I a "ghost" in that machine. Rather, I am a subjectively experiencing bodily insertion in the world. In fact, for Merleau-Ponty, the view that a person is either a machine or a "ghost" within it are abstractions and half-truths which presuppose the very reality of the lived body that each in its own way ignores.

It is within this context, then, that Merleau-Ponty

6. M. Pos, "Phénoménologie et Linguistique," *Revue International de Philosophie*, 1939.

comes to scrutinize language. In the process, he denies
any philosophy of language that would reduce it to an
act of the mind or a state of the (objective) body. Language is first of all a phenomenon of the lived world,
and Merleau-Ponty expresses this by referring to it in
the present tense as *speaking* (*la parole parlante*). In
fact, speaking is a form of "bodily gesture" or an expression of the dialectical bodily relation between me
and the world around me (as well as the past and the
future). As fear on my face is a bodily gesture which
expresses my bodily relation to an onrushing automo-
bile, so too speech is a sophisticated form of bodily
gesture expressing my relation to myself, the world about
me, and others. And just as the *Phenomenology of Perception* tries to clarify the lived relation of the subject
and the object in the bodily perceptual experience, so
the phenomenology of language attempts to return to
the speaking subject, i.e. the lived relation of a speaking
subject and the intended meanings of his speaking gestures within the act of speaking.[7] Speaking is the primary means for a person to order his lived world and
orient himself within it. As Kierkegaard put it, "the relief
of speech is that it translates me into the universal." [8]
The act of speaking in the context of the lived world
is the fundamental reality of language. Language is
neither a bodily motor-mechanism nor the expression of
pure mind. It is a lived expression of our bodily insertion
in the world.

And meaning is not detached from words. Words

7. M. Merleau-Ponty, "Sur la Phénoménologie du Langage,"
Problèmes Actuels de la Phénoménologie (ed. Van Breda), Paris,
1952, p. 102.
8. Soren Kierkegaard, *Fear & Trembling*, New York, 1953,
p. 122.

are not signs that refer elsewhere for their meaning. Rather, meaning is correlative to the speaker in the act of speaking. In speaking, we intend meaning, search for it perhaps, and then discover it in a word which expresses it. As a bodily gesture seeks its end in expression, so too speaking seeks a meaning which it more or less expresses in this or that vocal sound.[9] "The meaning of words must be finally induced by words themselves, or more exactly, their conceptual meaning must be formed by a kind of deduction from a *gestural meaning* which is immanent in speech."[10] We grasp meanings through words. Thus, no word sums up or fully realizes a meaning (note the poet's never-ending search for perfect expression). And this meaning doesn't exist apart from expression, but rather is carried into being by the gesture itself. The various forms of expression, but especially speech, are our only means of expressing or grasping meaning.[11] Further, since speaking expresses a meaning intended by a speaker, no word has one meaning alone. The meaning depends upon the intention of the speaker and the context of the expression, i.e. the meaning depends on its "usage." For example, the meaning of the word "love" in the statement, "I seek love," obviously depends upon *who* says it, his intentions, to *whom* he says it, and in general the context of the statement.

Words are not signs that refer to a single meaning. They are gestures expressive of our lived and bodily relation to the world and others. To reduce speech to a

9. M. Merleau-Ponty, *Signes,* Paris, 1960, p. 111.

10. *Phenomenology of Perception,* p. 179.

11. For further interesting insights on this problem, see James Edie, "Expression and Metaphor," *Philosophy and Phenomenological Research,* Vol. XXIII, 1963.

set of ideal meanings is to finalize one meaning of being. But being is not finished, and speech is not static and terminated in a single set of ideal meanings.[12] Meaning in speech is like the musical meaning of a sonata, inseparable from the notes that convey it.[13] We don't think first and then invent a language to express that thought. Nor do we listen to speech and then think the meaning. Thought and speaking are identical.

Finally, this gestural form of expression, speaking, becomes "sedimented" or "established" (*la parole parlante* becomes *la parole parlée*). Gestural vocal expressions—words—become familiar and commonplace, tools ready at hand for everyday discourse. And these "sedimented" meanings form the basis for the spoken languages of the many human tribes, peoples, and nations. From it emerge the cultures, the shared values and understandings, and the familiar social milieus and horizons of meaning of various peoples. Likewise, it is in terms of this "sedimented" speech that we are often led to think of language as signs referring to fixed meanings, as in the case of a dictionary for instance. Such is, of course, to ignore "usage." In phenomenological terms, it is to abstract the phenomenon of speech out of its lived context.

With that, let us turn more specifically to the present book, *Speaking*, and its author, Georges Gusdorf. Since this translation constitutes not only an existential and phenomenological philosophy of language but also the introduction of Gusdorf and his work to the American and English reader, it will be valuable to turn to a few of the more important details concerning his life and work to date.

12. *Signes*, p. 122.
13. *Phenomenology of Perception*, p. 182.

Professor Gusdorf received his philosophic training at France's most prestigious intellectual training ground, L'École Normale Supérieure. Although slightly younger, he came to know Maurice Merleau-Ponty fairly well and was acquainted with Jean Paul Sartre. He belongs to the generation of French philosophers that, from the early 1930's onward, was heavily influenced by the phenomenology of Edmund Husserl and Max Scheler and the existential thought of Heidegger, Kierkegaard, and Karl Jaspers. Thus, Gusdorf's philosophy developed parallel to the existentially oriented phenomenologies of Sartre, Merleau-Ponty, and Paul Ricoeur.

He became an instructor of philosophy at L'École Normale Supérieure just before the war, at the outbreak of which he was interned; he remained in captivity in Germany for four years. During those years he wrote two works, which were later published as *L'Expérience Humaine du Sacrifice* and *La Découverte de Soi*. After the war, he returned to L'École Normale Supérieure as an instructor. He remained there until 1949 when he became a professor at the University of Strasbourg, where he now resides.

Gusdorf is a prolific writer, and, since 1948, his bibliography has grown extensively.[14] The list of his

14. Other works by M. Gusdorf are:
La Découverte de Soi, Paris, 1948.
L'Expérience Humaine du Sacrifice, Paris, 1948.
Traité de L'Existence Morale, Paris, 1949.
Mémoire et Personne, Paris, 1951.
Mythe et Métaphysique, Paris, 1953.
Traité de Métaphysique, Paris, 1956.
La Vertu de Force, Paris, 1957.
Science et Foi, Paris, 1962.
Introduction aux Sciences Humaines, Strasbourg, 1961.
Signification Humaine de la Liberté, Paris, 1962.
Dialogue avec le Médicin, Paris, 1962.
Pourquoi des Professeurs?, Paris, 1963.

major publications is so long that we could not possibly analyze or summarize them for the reader in this introduction. Fortunately for us, however, there are, running throughout his books, a number of interrelated themes and interests. A bare mention of these themes, along with a few brief remarks and references to his works, may help the reader to orient this book within the total corpus of Gusdorf's philosophical writings.

First of all, M. Gusdorf is a member of the Reformed Church, and along with Paul Ricoeur of Paris (formerly of Strasbourg), Roger Mehl of Strasbourg, and the late Pierre Thévenaz of Lausanne, he is one of a group of Protestant philosophers attempting to work out a phenomenological and existential philosophy of religion. In fact, together with these philosophers, he has clearly found in the phenomenological method and the existential *a priori* of "lived existence" a radically new tool for coming to grips with religious experience in general and the Christian experience in particular. We see this throughout his works, whether in the form of an investigation of "myth," its place in the primitive world and its relation to metaphysics and philosophy (*Mythe et Métaphysique* and *Traité de Métaphysique*), religious self-sacrifice and personality integration (*L'Expérience Humaine du Sacrifice*) or the relation of faith and science (*Science et Foi*). In fact, it is this theme of Christian existentialism which makes Gusdorf a significant voice in contemporary French Protestant thought.

But it would be unfair to imply that Professor Gusdorf's interests lie exclusively in the area of Christian apologetics or even the general field of the philosophy of religion. This is certainly not true. In fact, his interests cover all of the problems and interests of existential phenomenology.

It is clear from his writings that Gusdorf's fundamental starting point is the primary existential reality of "lived existence" or "concrete experience." He accepts the phenomenological conception of "intentionality" to characterize this personal experience or lived existence. A man is a being-to-the-world. The *Lebenswelt* or the field of correlative experience *is* reality to the existing subject. Gusdorf's primary interest, then, is to treat such phenomena of human existence as freedom, memory, time, and other persons, within the horizon of this concrete and "worldly" experience. And knowledge of this personal reality in all its richness and variety consists of a descriptive (and thus phenomenological) analysis of the various phenomena which constitute it. This double theme of the *a priori* of our personal experience in the world along with the phenomenological method of description characterizes Gusdorf, then, as an existential phenomenologist, and pervades all of his work. We see it in his phenomenological descriptions of time and memory in *Mémoire et Personne;* we see it in the description of self-affirmation and creation in *La Découverte de Soi;* and we see it in his treatment of human freedom in *Signification Humaine de la Liberté.*

A third theme which runs throughout his works is his interest in ethics. The reader will see indications of this in his reference to "value" in *Speaking.* But besides being a theme woven into the very texture of his books, it is also the subject of a book, *Traité de L'Existence Morale;* two other works, *L'Expérience Humaine du Sacrifice* and *La Vertu de Force,* deal, at least in part, with an analysis of ethical experience. This side of Professor Gusdorf's work constitutes perhaps his most interesting and genuinely original contribution to philosophy. For those who so often ask, "what of existential ethics?" we can recommend Gusdorf's original and soundly-based work in this realm of existential phenomenology.

For the rest, Gusdorf's interests range as far afield as, for example, a study of the social sciences, the nature of the human world and the place of science within it (*Introduction aux Sciences Humaines*), metaphysics (*Traité de Métaphysique*), and indeed all the problems and fields traditionally associated with philosophy. His work constitutes, in fact, an impressive body of philosophic reflection.

But what of this book, *Speaking*? It was originally published in 1953 in a series edited by Jean Lacroix at the *Presses Universitaires de France*, a series entitled *Initiation Philosophique*. It was intended to be an introduction to the philosophy of language for the general, educated French reader. The French philosopher, Henry Duméry, calls it *"un petit chef-d'oeuvre,"* which "provides in some ways the model of what a series devoted to the introduction of philosophy ought to be." [15]

This is, then, an introduction to the philosophy of language from an existential and phenomenological point of view. Rather than a technically finished and complete phenomenology of language, it is intended to be a non-technical and yet sophisticated introduction to that already growing field of interest within existential phenomenology.

One thing ought to be emphasized, here. From the initial pages dealing with the central role played by speech within human reality to the final pages dealing with an "ethic" of speech, Gusdorf's central concern is to analyze speech within the context of human reality.

15. H. Duméry, *Regards Sur la Philosophie Contemporaine*, Paris, 1957, p. 220.

Speech is not the problem, he tells us at one point, but speaking men—i.e., the act of speaking. Speech is an abstraction, but speaking is not. Living men speak, and that activity reflects the being of the speaker in that it is the means whereby he constitutes himself and human culture against the mute background of nature. Speaking expresses the experiential and dialectical relation of man, nature, and society. In other words, it is through speaking that nature is sublimated into the meant and expressive world of human reality. Speech displays the wondrous power of men to give meaning to themselves and the world by expressing their lived insertion and active engagement in nature, history, and society. The pursuit of that insight, and all the implications and problems it leads to, constitutes the basic concern of this book.

PAUL T. BROCKELMAN

Durham, New Hampshire
January 1965

Definitions

Language is a psychological function corresponding to the activation of a collection of anatomical and physiological potentialities. It extends into perspectives of mind systematized in a complex total exercise, and it is characteristic only of human beings.

A *tongue* is the system of spoken expression peculiar to a human community. The exercise of language produces in the long run a kind of sedimentary deposit, which takes on the value of an institution and imposes itself upon individual speech in the matter of vocabulary and grammar.

Speaking denotes human reality as it evolves, from day to day, in expression. It is no longer a psychological function nor a social reality, but an affirmation of the person in the moral and metaphysical order.

Language and the tongue are abstract data, conditions for the possibility of speech, which incorporates them, assuming them in order to actualize them. Only speaking men exist—men capable of a language and situated within the horizon of a tongue. Thus, there is a hierarchy of signification. It stretches from the simple vocal sound, which is stylized into a word through the imposition of a social meaning, to affective human speaking which bears particular intentions that are the vehicles of personal values.

[xxix]

Contents

Translator's Introduction / xi
Definitions / xxix

   I · Speaking as the Threshold of the
      Human World   3
  II · Speaking and the Gods: Theology of
      Language   11
 III · Speaking and the Philosophers   19
 IV · Speaking as Human Reality   35
  V · Speaking as Encounter   47
 VI · Communication   61
 VII · Expression   69
VIII · The Authenticity of Communication 77
 IX · The World of Speaking   93
  X · Homo Loquens   99
 XI · Techniques of Stabilizing Speech   109
 XII · Toward an Ethic of Speech   119

Short Bibliography / 129
Index of Names / 131
[xxxi]

Speaking
(La Parole)

I / Speaking as the Threshold
of the Human World

A CHARACTER portrayed by Diderot in the discussions following the *Rêve de d'Alembert* imagines "in a glass cage in the Royal Gardens, an orangutan with the air of a Saint John praying in the desert." The cardinal of Polignac, admiring the creature one day, is supposed to have said to him: "speak and I will baptize you." These words of a witty clergyman, reported by an unbelieving literateur, doubtless go much further than the writer or the speaker himself thought. It was a question of making clear the small distance between beast and mankind, a mankind that believes itself so superior and thinks that it can increase its worth even more by virtue of the sacrament. Diderot here anticipates the argument against man's pretentions to superiority that certain Darwinians will later draw from the theory of evolution. The break between beast and person is infinitesimal. In fact, all that the animal lacks is speech.

True. However, the orangutan didn't answer the cardinal. He did not utter the key word which would have definitively made him cross the threshold from animality to humanity. Language is the necessary and sufficient condition for entrance into the human world. An ancient anecdote pictures a shipwrecked philosopher cast up by a storm on an unknown shore. He notices a few geometric figures traced in the sand by a passer-by. Turning to his companions, he says: "We are safe; I perceive here the mark of man." Mathematical symbolization, *the* language in which all men communicate beyond the diversity of idioms, is the highest testimony to the establishment of man on earth. Animals speak only in fairy tales. And that's why men, since they learned to speak, have been able to domesticate animals, while animals have never succeeded in domesticating man.

Man is the speaking animal: this definition, after so many others, is perhaps the most decisive one. It overlaps and absorbs such traditional definitions of man as the animal who laughs, or the social animal. For human laughter testifies to an interior language within oneself, and between oneself and others. Likewise, to say that man is a political animal, when social creatures exist, means that human relations are founded upon language. Speech isn't involved simply to facilitate these relations; it constitutes them. The universe of discourse has covered over and transfigured the material environment.

But to say that language provides the password for entrance into the human world is to pose a problem and not to resolve it. Nothing is more paradoxical in fact than the appearance of language in man. Anatomy and physiology only furnish, here, fragmentary and insufficient explanations. A scientist from outer space, limiting himself to the examination of the remains of man and the superior apes, would probably not discern that capital difference between man and the chimpanzee, whose bodies are so similar. If he did not know it by some other means, he would not discover that the function of language exists in man and is lacking in the ape.

Speech appears as a function without a specific and exclusive organ that would allow for its localization. A certain number of anatomical dispositions contribute to it, but they are dispersed throughout the organism, and are bound together for the single purpose of an activity which superimposes itself upon them without mixing them together. We speak with our vocal cords, but only because we have certain cerebral structures as well, and the vocal cords must function in conjunction with the lungs, the tongue, the whole mouth and even the auditory apparatus—for the congenitally deaf man is necessarily speechless. Now, all the elements of speech exist in the superior ape, but, even if he achieves the emission of sounds, he is nevertheless incapable of language.

The mystery here has to do with an extension of natural potentialities, with their coordination in a higher and properly emergent (*surnaturel*) order. If the chimpanzee has the potential for language, but not its reality, then the function of speech in its essence is not an organic function at all, but a function of the mind and spirit. Scientists have tried to circumvent the mystery as much as possible, and to distinguish man and animal by means of myriad experiments. Both have been submitted to a series of carefully controlled tests. Even better, they have gone as far as to raise to maturity, side by side and in identical conditions, a baby monkey and a human infant, so as to follow in detail the development of their several functions. Their beginnings are apparently the same. The human and the baby chimpanzee utilize analogous resources to become established in their progressively disclosed worlds. From 9 to 18 months, the contest between the two rivals remains a tie. They respond to the same tests with varying success, the one or the other indicating his superiority according to the circumstances. The infant monkey is without doubt more adroit; the human infant is capable of relatively more sustained attention.

But quite soon the moment comes when the development of the monkey stops, whereas that of the infant takes a new lease on life. The comparison becomes meaningless: the monkey is obviously merely an animal; the baby has access to human reality. The line which finally absolutely separates them is the threshold of language. The chimpanzee can emit certain sounds, uttering cries of pleasure or pain, but these vocal gestures remain tied to emotion in him. He does not know how to make use of them independently of the situation in which they occur. The most elaborate training only ends in poor results: the mechanical repetition of the parakeet or the conditioned reflex created in an animal that responds automatically to a given signal, such as a dog's barking on command.

The child on the other hand starts on a slow educational process which will make of him a new being in a transformed world. This apprenticeship, stretched over many years, is based on the association of voice and hearing at the service of a novel function, the possibilities of which infinitely transcend those of the elementary senses so united within it. Human intelligence uses and synthesizes the sensory-motor structures by the affirmation of a higher end. We ought to notice this emergence and admit that it does not take place in the animal, within which the voice is never freed from lived totality and allied with the auditory sense. We cannot explain this dissociation and association except by a vocation in man peculiar to humanity, a vocation which progressively gives to the new function of speech an undeniable preponderance in behavior. It is here, in the hierarchy of living beings, that we must draw the line of demarcation that separates man from animal—a separation brought about by a decisive mutation.

The advent of the word manifests the sovereignty of man. Man interposes a network of words between the world and himself and thereby becomes the master of the world.

The animal doesn't understand *sign*, but only *signal*, that is to say the conditioned reaction to a situation recognized in its global form, but not analyzed in its detail. Its conduct aims at adaptation to a concrete presence to which it adheres through its needs, its awakened senses. These are the only symbols for it, the only intelligible elements presented by an event it doesn't control, but in which it participates. The human word intervenes like an abstract of the situation. It permits a breaking-up of the situation and a perpetuation of it, in other words an escape from the constraint of the present in order to take up a position in the security of distance and absence.

The animal world thus appears as a succession of always present and constantly disappearing situations, defined solely by their reference to the biological requirements of the organism. On the other hand, the human world presents itself as an ensemble of objects, i.e. stable elements of reality, independent of the context of the particular situations in which they may manifest themselves. Beyond an instinctive and momentary reality offered to the very spontaneous moment of awareness, an ideational reality is fashioned, more stable and true than appearance. Objects which resist desire become the center of situations instead of always being subordinate to them. The word is more important than the thing, it exists at a higher level. The human world is no longer a world of sensations and reactions, but a universe of designations and ideas.

It's important to feel wonder before this discovery of the word, leading as it does to human reality beyond the simple animal environment. The power of a name is indicated by the fact that it gives *identity* to a thing. Language condenses in itself that human power which permits the elucidation of thoughts by the elucidation of things. Structures of mind (*les structures intellectuelles*) emerge from the confusion; it is on their level henceforth that the most effective action takes place, action at a distance and the negation of that distance.

Nothing better illumines the privileged place of language in the constitution of the world than the negative proof realized in diseases of language. An aphasiac, in whom the mechanisms of speech are affected, is not simply deprived of a certain number of words, and incapable of correctly designating them. This aspect of his illness, long considered primary, is in fact only secondary. The aphasiac is a man in whom the linguistic function is breaking down; the whole intellectual structuring of existence within him is in the process of collapsing. He loses the sense of the unity and identity of an object. In a fragmented and incoherent world, he is captive of the concrete situation, condemned to a kind of vegetable life. Therefore, properly speaking, there are no illnesses of language, but only personality disorders. The patient finds himself divorced from human reality, and, so to speak, fallen away from that world into which the emergence of speech had caused him to enter. Terms that gather identical objects or qualities under one label no longer are able to exercise their disciplinary function. Everything which language had given, aphasia takes back. This grim destruction of personal life thus excludes one from the human community.

Properly speaking, language does not create the world; objectively, the world is already there. The power of language however is to constitute, where incoherent sensations leave off, a universe to the measure of man. Each individual who comes into the world resumes for himself that labor of the human species, essential to it from its inception. To come into the world is *to begin speaking (prendre la parole)*, to transfigure experience into a universe of discourse. According to a famous maxim of Marx found in the eleventh of the *Theses on Feuerbach,* "philosophers have simply interpreted the world in different ways; what counts is to transform it." In that respect one may say that the appearance of language has been more than a philosophy, more than a simple transcription. It has signified an overturning of the conditions of existence, a reworking of the environment for the establishment of man.

The word owes its efficacy to the fact that it is not an objective notation, but an *index of value.* The most common name does not limit its activity to the object it denotes by appearing to isolate it from its context; it determines the object as a function of its environment. It crystallizes reality, it condenses it into a function of an attitude of the person. It exercises an implicit choice in the wake of a global intention. In other words, each word is *a situation-word* (*le mot de la situation*), the word which sums up the state of the world as a function of my decision. Undoubtedly the objectivity of established language ordinarily hides this personal sense. However the real word is much less an in-itself than a for-myself. It implies a projection of the world, a world in project. Thus it is that the value of language is not distinguished, when all is said and done, from the value of the world. Speech is not merely rich with ideas. It recovers and assumes all orientations, intentions, desires, and inner disciplines at their birth. Consciousness, ineffective as long as it remains isolated, bursts forth toward the world, bursts forth into the form of the world, revealing the world to man and disclosing man to the world. Language is the being of man carried to self-awareness—the overture to transcendence.

The invention of language is thus the first of the great inventions, that which contains all the others in germ. It is perhaps less sensational than the domestication of fire, but more decisive. Language manifests itself as the original of the many human techniques. It constitutes an economical means of manipulating entities and things. Often a word grasps reality more and better than does a tool or a weapon. For speech constitutes the building blocks of the universe, and it goes on to re-educate the natural world. Thanks to it, the natural world becomes the emergent human reality (*la surréalité humaine*), consonant with the power that brought it into being. Orpheus, the first of all poets, charmed, with his incantations, animals, plants, and the very stones which obeyed his voice. Myth here restores to us the meaning of human speech, a speech which imposes its authority on the universe.

II / Speaking and the Gods:
Theology of Language

IF IT IS ESTABLISHED that the power of speech is so decisive, it is certainly necessary to admit that it takes on a character which goes beyond the possibilities of man. The philanthropic gods of Greek mythology had endowed the human species with wheat, the olive tree, and the vine; likewise, the gift of language must have a divine origin. But even more, the first word, in its transcendent efficacy, is bound up with the establishment of humanity; the first word is the very *calling* of man to be human. This first word must have been the Word of God, a word that is the creator of the human order. Word of grace, a call to be, an appeal to human beings, the first word is thus the essence which includes existence, which calls existence forth.

This prototype of speech in its fullness is universally imposed on consciousness, from its lowest to its most sophisticated forms. The primacy of a divine Word is everywhere asserted, a word that is then communicated to man who is still completely enveloped in its transcendent meaning. The first language is essential language; it has a magical and religious value. It is not simply designation, but an immanent reality by virtue of which it is possible for man to repeat the denominative and at the same time creative act of God, and to carry off for his own profit the powers which it brings into play.

The meaning of a name among primitive peoples is linked to the very being of the thing named. The word doesn't act as a label more or less arbitrarily added beyond the thing. It contains in itself the revelation of the thing itself in its most intimate nature. To know the name is to have power over the thing. For example, a primitive tribe of the Dutch East Indies possesses a system of medicine which relies entirely on the names of illnesses and remedies. Plants and substances will be used the names of which evoke health or recovery, and avoided are those names which make one think of disease. It is as if in America one used a leaf of the Sweet Gum tree to heal a disease of the gums, or Passion fruit for patients suffering from frigidity. The pun is used because the play on words indicates a manipulation on the level of being itself. Given such a point of view, it is easy to understand the necessity for a rigorous hygiene, a prophylaxis of names. It is most important to protect the ontological identity of things and persons from the foreigner, the enemy. The real name will be kept secret since it is a password for getting at a life which, being defenseless, is open to hostile enterprises. The gods themselves are helpless before the power of whoever calls them by their names. The simple, thoughtless use of a word can entail disastrous consequences. Man and god, therefore, will be designated in ordinary usage by false, harmless names. The real names—protected by the mysterious rites of initiation—are reserved for magical and religious rites, and entrusted only to specialists, sorcerers or priests, and initiates.

The field of name magic seems immense. It extends to primitive man in general. Moreover, it reappears at the beginning of every person's life, for the childhood of each man repeats that of humanity in general. M. Piaget has described a period of *nominal realism* in which the child who has just achieved speech gives to that instrument a miraculous value. To know the name of a thing is to have grasped its essence. Hence the feverish questions of the child avid to know "what's that called?", since for him it is a means of appropriating all that he is capable of naming. Thus, here again the word is the summons to be, thought activates a reality from which it is never dissociated.

The first man then appears to be he for whom language remains under the domination of this ontological union. That confused awareness of the primitive does not disappear when new forms of civilization come into being. Intellectual expression is perfected, but the intention remains identical. The great religions all make room for a doctrine of the divine Word in the establishment of reality. In ancient Egypt, the demiurge created the world by pronouncing the names of creatures and things. The sovereign word suffices to constitute all of reality by the mere expression of the name. Egyptian wisdom compares the commandment of the Pharaoh to the divine Word. The king speaks and all things are made as he has said, by means of the force of sacred character inherent in the person of the monarch. In Hindu spirituality, the same word designates at once the name, the body, and the form of man. A Vedic hymn teaches that speech was created by the seven sages who founded sacrifice, the center of all religious life. Sacrifice itself has as an end "to follow in the footsteps of speech." Brahmanism has even summed up all of its spiritual discipline with one key word—the syllable *om*—not merely a designation, but a symbol of being, an expression of supreme reality in its highest mystical presence. To understand this syllable is to transcend the human condition and to lose oneself in the divine identity.

The traditional wisdom of China has excluded any religious affirmation, properly speaking. However, in this ethical outlook, this way of life, language assumes a vast significance because the order of words implies the order of things. The universe presents itself as a coherent discourse, and it is important that each person religiously respect its organization. A doctrine attributed to Confucius says: "Good order depends entirely upon correctness of language." If language goes awry, the universe is in danger of being off-balance. Further, Confucius remarks:

> "If designations are not correct, words won't fit together; if words won't fit together, political affairs have no success; if political affairs have no success, neither rites nor music flourishes . . . punishments and chastisements are unjustly meted out, and people do not know how to act. Thus it is that the sage, when he names things, sees to it that words conform to reality, and, when he uses them, he sees to it that they are actualized in the practical world."

This text strikingly reveals the transcendent power of human speech. Words have a consistency which involves the meaning of the universe: good usage contributes to the movement of the world as to the celebration of cosmic harmony. The emperor Che Houang-ti, in order to establish his authority and consolidate peace, standardizes writing, publishes an official dictionary and, proud of his work, proclaims on his statue: "I have brought order to the masses and I have tested acts and realities: each thing has the name which is proper to it." In the same way Richelieu in France will prepare the way for absolute monarchy by founding the Academy, an institution responsible for defining a code of good usage by promulgating a dictionary and a grammar. Nearer to home, it was astonishing recently to see the head of the Soviet state play the philologist in a document in which he took a position on the problem of the future of human tongues, foreseeing the progressive unification of varying idioms. The reason is that the establishment of an empire must have a corresponding centralization of language. Any important reform, any revolution demands a renewal of vocabulary. Men have not been transformed so long as their way of speaking has remained unchanged.

This intimate tie between language and the being of the world and man, in whatever form it is experienced, appears then as a constant characteristic of the human consciousness of values. The sacred books of Christianity likewise affirm the divine significance of language. It is the Word of God that called the world into being. God speaks, and things are; the Word is in itself creative. The sense of that ontological word remains present on the horizon of Christian thought, as a goal to be fulfilled. The Christian Revelation is nothing else than the Word of God, just as the holy scriptures express it. And Jesus Christ, the Son of God who brings about a spiritual rebirth of humanity, is presented as the Word made flesh. He is the Word of God made man, at work on the earth, in the fullness of His power opening the eyes of the blind and resurrecting the dead.

Furthermore, there is in the Bible a whole theology of names corresponding to this ontology of language. The God of Christianity is a hidden God; no name discloses his essence to us. Such is already the teaching of the Old Testament, which shows us the Omnipotent revealing Himself to Moses and introducing Himself under the name of the famous Hebrew tetragram, *Yahweh* (mistakenly written as *Jehovah*). Now this name of God is not a name at all, but only a statement of existence, a verbal form signifying simply: *He is*. Man cannot know the name of God because to know this name would be for the created to find himself equal to his Creator. Only the Creator knows the names of the beings which He has created—in other words there is nothing hidden in them for Him. On Sinai, the Eternal says to Moses: "I know thee by name. . . ." [1] And when Jesus at the beginning of his ministry imposes a new name on one of his first disciples, he says: "Thou art Simon the son of Jonah: thou shalt be called Cephas." [2] This change of name represents the *calling* of Peter; it consecrates the conversion of the apostle, called by the new name to a new life. Besides, in the strict Christian tradition the real name of a person is the baptismal name given to the child on behalf of God. The weakening of the Christian name in favor of the family name is a sign of modern de-Christianization.

Thus, a man should serve God in the world by respecting His word. Human language, guaranteed by divine Providence, was thought to assure order in piety. Now the book of Genesis very early shows us humanity

1. Exodus 33:12.
2. John 1:42.

divided against itself, and thereby in a state of igno-
rance with respect to the pre-established harmony of
creation. Sacred history is presented as a series of diso-
bediences in which the original transgression is endlessly multiplied. The episode of the tower of Babel
symbolizes this decline of the peoples forgetful of the
divine word. "And the whole earth was of one language,
and of one speech." [3] But God, in order to punish the
prideful excess of the human enterprise, puts a brake
on the whole project by bringing about the confusion of
tongues. The unitary language of creation is replaced
by the diversity of the tongues of sin which make men
strangers to one another. "Because the Lord did there
confound the language of all the earth: and from
thence did the Lord scatter them abroad upon the face
of all the earth." [4] And since then, those who dream of
the reconciliation of all the world, whether they be
Christian or not, seek a universal Esperanto. They seek
a global tongue whose universality would have the mar-
velous power to resolve the age-old misunderstanding
of human wickedness.

But the tower of Babel is not the last word in the
Christian doctrine of language. Another episode in the
New Testament echoes the tragedy of Genesis. It is
the revelation of Pentecost, the Holy Spirit descending
upon the apostles and giving to them the gift of
tongues. Thus, the early breakdown is compensated by
the mystical return to unity. Not that one should imagine the apostles suddenly endowed with polyglot and
encyclopedic knowledge. The meaning is doubtless that
the disciple of Christ possesses that power to reconcile
in himself the diversity of men, and to discover that

3. Genesis 11:1.
4. Genesis 11:9.

word which suits every individual, being a means to penetrate the secret depths of his soul. The plurality of tongues continues. It is overcome only in intention. It is overcome in the hope of Christian faith.

Christian thought has thus profoundly posed the problems of language. It has shown the gulf between the Word of God and the word of man. It itself has oscillated between the speech of Babel, proud and damned, and the speech of grace, the redeemed speech of Pentecost. The rejection of a transcendent speech and the discovery of the relativity of language marks an important date in the spiritual life of humanity. Babel repeats the exodus from the earthly paradise. The pre-established harmony of the Garden of Eden corresponded to the dogmatic sleep of innocence before the Fall. Man relied on the guarantees of mythical consciousness in a universe without problems, every aspect of which spoke to him of divine intentions. After the Fall, after Babel, man finds himself the master of a disenchanted language. For better or for worse he himself must assume responsibility for it. Speech is no longer guaranteed by the providential predestination which had been crystallizing it into a superhuman order. At the level of mythical consciousness, there is only a single language, a divine language, which actualizes the unity of the world. There is only one world because there is only one way of speaking. All problems are resolved because they are never raised. The catastrophe of Babel opens to human activity the enterprise of reflection and freedom.

III / Speaking and the
Philosophers

THE SYMBOLIC LINE of demarcation is thus
that of the commonly held notion that the word does
not stand on its own, but depends on us. The human
domain becomes detached from ontology. A moment of
astonishment, of disenchantment, of disquietude: that
is when philosophy emerges. Man begins to see that in
spite of all mythical prohibitions, he can meddle with
those words which until then had subjugated him to
their law. Words wait for their justification to come
from him. A transfer of power establishes that discovery. The mythical world was a world of denominations
with a name for everything, and with everything existing according to its name. The world of reflection, on
the other hand, is a world of meaning: denominations
are worthless without intentions.

The adventure of Western thought begins when
Greek reflection throws into relief the autonomy of
human speech. It is part of the nature of man to create
according to the realities of nature, at least the meaning of those realities. By that means, man, the measure

of all things, is a god in his universe, a god who bargains with the gods, and who presumes to dispute with them the possession of the world. Greek rhetoric and sophistry testify to the fact that the world in which we live is a world of speech, that the clever man can compose at will in order to trick others. From that time on, creativity confines man to impiety since it denies to truth all transcendent value, and from now on only allows an all-too-human technique to take its place. Over against that threatening anarchy there now arises the protest of Socrates who tries to save human unity by a radical exegesis of discourse. "Words do not belong to us," Socrates protests, "as prey to our whim." The clarification of words is necessary as an examination of conscience. The categorical imperative to be correct with terms coincides with the duty to be faithful to oneself and obedient to the gods.

Plato and Aristotle will extend the Socratic effort towards a unity rediscovered through the convergence of human meanings. Immediate experience is that of disorder. But the intervention of thought brings out that return to harmony which is a rediscovery of the divine. Such, in effect, is the start of Platonic reflection: the *Cratylus,* one of the most important of the earlier dialogues, has as a goal, as the subtitle indicates, the "rightness of words." Philology is certainly the beginning of philosophy. It will drive from the temple of wisdom the Sophists—illusionists and tricksters—who, mixing truth and falsehood at will, destroy all wisdom and piety. The Socratic method is presented as an inquiry into vocabulary: what is courage? justice? piety? The questioned one at first replies with assurance, proposing this or that banal formula, which Socrates shows without trouble is contradictory and meaningless. *Common sense* is a bad teacher; it is necessary to abandon it in order to return to *good sense*. Reflection, under the sting of Socratic irony, brings into play in everyone the mediation of a more profound judgment, the master of Truth beyond appearance. It thus appears that the most simple words are nevertheless indications of being, revelations to us of a genuine Thought which transcends our thought and authenticates it.

The principle work of Greek philosophy has thus had as its goal the giving of a language to truth. The Platonic doctrine of ideas unites the world of words and appearances with a world of transcendent forms. Human thought is saved since dialectic permits the human to invoke the surety of the divine. Aristotle will substitute for the Platonic ideas conceptual essences to which man has direct access by means of an appropriate intuition. Speech will be justified by the establishment of metaphysics, in triumphant reply to the criticism of the Sophists. But that metaphysical speech has forever lost the massive innocence of pre-reflective mythical speech. Mythical speech had been presented until then as a divine monologue. The discipline of language consisted for man in the respect for transcendent order. The new ontology, however, is presented as a *dialogue*, in other words as a piece of common labor and, at the same time, debate. It is a dialogue in which Socrates the gadfly initially takes one of the two sides, but soon comes to efface himself. It is a dialogue of each with himself, a dialogue of reason with the gods. Such is the meaning of *dialectic* in which a growing participation of the human mind in the activity of speech is indicated. The radical humanism of the Sophists, which had proclaimed freedom from all transcendent norms, results, amongst those who maintained the primacy of truth against relativism, in a kind of activation of ontology which propagates itself as concepts, as ideas, and within which the monolithic being of the primitives is parcelled out.

At the same time, the awareness that there is an activity of human judgment becomes established, called upon to make certain that language participates in being. Truth, at the level of speech, must be built up and ceaselessly subjected to criticism. Man has jurisdiction over words: it's up to him to bring them into line with reality. Ancient thought brings together within itself an ontological realism of the concept and an intellectualistic idealism of the judgment, the marriage of which was then torn apart—the problem of language becoming thus *the* problem of metaphysics. That preoccupation appears at the very center of medieval thought, which can be understood as an immense debate on the theme of the ontological validity of human speech. Various schools try to resolve the problem of universals: what is the nature of the general ideas to which the words we use refer? Are there, in order to give consistency to our words, transcendent spiritual realities, Platonic ideas, essences—or rather are concepts nothing other than the words that designate them? Does a humanity exist distinct from concrete men, or is humanity simply a name? Between the conceptualist ontologism and the nominalist nihilism, a spectrum of very subtle positions defines various orientations of mind.

These vague disputes astonish us today by the passion they aroused concerning a seemingly purely verbal problem. But the reason is that the very foundations of metaphysics and theology are cast in doubt over the meanings of words. If only individuals exist, if the genera are only names, then the three Persons of the Trinity can never coincide, and we are victims of polytheism. Likewise with the Fall of Adam. If it is the Fall of a man and not of humanity, then it could not have been passed on, and the dogma of original sin becomes contradictory. But conversely, if the genus exists, individuals are obliterated. The singular reality of each man is dissolved into universal humanity, and now a new heresy threatens, that of pantheism. The vigilance of the learned doctors must remain constantly alert. Each word implies a creed, and the threat of excommunication hangs over those who, in playing with words, risk the destruction of Christianity.

These overly subtle word-games of scholasticism finally had to arouse the distrust and hostility of the best minds. On the pretext of interpreting the word of God, it is in fact a revived sophistry that emerges in the sterile debates of the School. They are debates in which intellectual houses of cards are built according to elaborate rituals of argument. Thereby, by dint of formulas and arguments, the learned doctors confuse everything. They lose touch with the God of the Gospels and the world of experience. If one seeks to rediscover the road to faith, wisdom, and truth, he must start over again from the beginning—in other words create a new tongue. Every spiritual or intellectual revolution demands a previous transformation of the established language. The Renaissance and Reformation are particularly outstanding examples of this.

The immense upheaval of the Renaissance, indeed, finds in the birth of modern philology not only its symbol, but perhaps its essence. The learned henceforth are no longer theologians and debaters, but the men of letters, erudite men who set out to revive dead languages. First of all, Latin: now, there is a living Latin, Church Latin, mother tongue of the liturgy and of scholasticism. The humanists assert that this idiom is a decadent form of Latin. Beyond low medieval Latin, they recommend the return to Ciceronian purity. The study of Latin henceforth is complemented by the study of Greek, neglected by the Western Church. And classical philology, having become a rigorous discipline which beyond words involves men and civilizations, even makes room for Semitic studies in the new College de France—a lay institution created beside the traditional colleges and medieval faculties.

There is much more involved in this than merely remodeling the curriculum of higher education. The new understanding of ancient language enlarges the horizons of thought: the creation of philology is here a sort of equivalent to the great discoveries which, in the same period, by modifying the structures of the world, prepare that new self-consciousness characteristic of modern man. Whole continents, unknown because forgotten, are opened to the learned: the Hebrew Old Testament and the Greek New Testament are extricated, in all their freshness, from the sedimented strata in which the Latin Church had deposited them. Direct access to the sacred texts in their original tongues opens the way to a new understanding of the Christian revelation. This rediscovery is accompanied by a shock effect, destined long to reverberate throughout human awareness.

But by an unexpected upset, this revolution, which rediscovers in Holy Scripture the Word of the living God, manifests itself as a revolution with a double effect on the level of language. Latin, which loses the privilege of being the mother tongue of the sacred texts, also ceases to be the tongue for communicating and teaching them. The revelation of the return to the sources for the learned is accompanied for the simple faithful by that other revelation, which constitutes direct access to the Scriptures: translation into the vulgar tongues. The Reformation, for the needs of the spiritual life, brings about as well the birth of modern German and English, the first monuments of which are the Lutheran and Anglican Bibles. Henceforth, each of the faithful can pray to God and read His Word in his own tongue.

As a result, the fall of Latin symbolizes for the West the breakup of medieval Christianity before the thrust of modern nationalities. Spiritual fragmentation bears witness to political disunion. The dream of "Romania," of catholic universality, ends with the renewal of the disaster of Babel. Men understand one another less and less; theology no longer speaks the tongue of a unified world. But, by an extraordinary coincidence, the very moment of that failure coincides with the surging forth of a new hope. A language arises that seems capable of reconciling minds in the universality of an authentic ecumenism. Galileo, brilliant prophet of an emerging tradition, declares: "Mathematics is the language in which the universe is written." Mathematics, indeed, transcends the confusion of tongues and nationalities. It substitutes for the doubtful subtlety of the Scholastic theological jargon an absolute rigor, an examplary concatenation of formulas and ideas.

A veritable revolution in knowledge is thus indicated, in the coming of that philology of nature made possible by recourse to mathematics. Nature speaks in a coded language; God, as Plato had long since said, is the geometer of eternity. In order to reach Him, the surest way is to decipher the order He has put into creation. The modern philosopher is a geometer and a technician, like Kepler, Descartes, or Newton, illuminating the strict laws that manifest the divine plan of the world. Henceforth, *the* language of all truth will be that of mathematical reasoning. Descartes, in well-known words, praises the excellence of "those long, completely simple and clear chains of argument which geometers are accustomed to use to achieve the most difficult demonstrations." [1] Such is from now on the model for all philosophic thought. For example, Spinoza, composing a metaphysical treatise, presents it in geometric order—like a chain of theorems deduced the one from the other.

There is thus a language of reason. In the place of the fallen authority of the Church and tradition the new authority of a critical consciousness is substituted, clarifying each of its words in order to progress step by step into the full light. The whole task of philosophy is simply to elaborate that perfect language in which each term will be clear and distinct, and whose very movement will obey intelligible principles. The meaning of the Cartesian reform consists in perfecting this rigorous language, thereby giving philosophy an instrument as sure in the order of thought as the new mathematics is in the order of figures and numbers. A curious letter of the young Descartes testifies to this. On November 20, 1629, he replies to his correspondent, Mersenne, who had communicated to him a project for a universal language—a kind of Esperanto proposed by a scholar of the time. The project in question doesn't seem to be worthwhile to him; it is the work of a philologist who is content merely to coin and catalogue words. An au-

1. Descartes, *Discourse on Method*, Part 2.

thentic universal language on the other hand must be the very language of reason, expressing not things but true ideas.

Descartes goes on:

> "The invention of that language depends on true philosophy. It is impossible otherwise to enumerate all the thoughts of men and to put them in order or even to separate them so that they are clear and simple, which in my opinion is the greatest secret that one may have for acquiring solid knowledge."

The whole enterprise of the *Discourse on Method* is found here in germ; and it is clear that it has no other ambition than to give to human reason the symbolic language of science. This universal language, continues Descartes, will be easy to learn. It will aid the judgment.

> "Instead of that, we now have the contrary. The words we have scarcely have anything but confused meanings. Because the mind of man has long become accustomed to them, it understands almost nothing perfectly. Now I hold that that language is possible, that one can discover the knowledge upon which it depends, and that by means of it peasants would be better able to judge the truth of things than philosophers now do. . . ."

In the place of this confused and fantastic language of common sense it is necessary, then, to substitute the rigorous language of good sense, enlightened by the intuitive evidence born of submission to reason. One may say that the entire work of Descartes will be merely the carrying-out of this program of his youth. It is a gigantic effort to subject to the unity and universality of one single language man, the world and God, metaphysics, science and technology. Of course, the undertaking was not to be completely fulfilled. Its full success would have meant going beyond the human condition, a kind of end of history. Man, the possessor of the key words of the universe, would thus take the place of God. From the time of the letter about language to Fr. Mersenne, the young Descartes seemed to be conscious of this impossibility. The universal language is realizable, he declares, "but never expect to see it in use; that presumes great changes in the order of things, and would necessitate that the whole world be simply a terrestrial paradise, a proposition limited to fiction." Thus the highest accomplishment of reason remains utopian. Humanity still finds itself under the sign of Babel. Descartes himself, one of the most intrepid of those who affirm reason, does not believe in the ultimate success of that language, to the creation of which he does, however, dedicate his life. Universal language indeed would mean a perfection of knowledge and a humanity reconciled in peace forever.

The letter of Descartes nevertheless remains the creed of modern thought. It is a document of such importance that Leibniz, another genius who was likewise to dream of the universal language, copied it in his own handwriting and kept it in his papers. The followers of Descartes remain faithful to this plan for the triumph of reason, but they free themselves from the metaphysical presuppositions to which the master's thought remained faithful. The *Rules for the Direction of the Mind* and the *Discourse on Method* ascribe a great deal to man's effort in building up knowledge. But the very elements of it are borrowed from a transcendent reality. The simple natures of Descartes, the clear and distinct ideas, like the Platonic ideas or the concepts of Aristotle before, correspond to ontological assumptions.

Human geometry is the repetition of a divine geometry; man deciphers the plan of God. Undoubtedly the God of Descartes, without ever patently contradicting the God of the Bible, still doesn't seem to maintain very intimate relations with Him. Nevertheless the God of the philosophers and scientists still appears as the arbiter of human endeavors, the limits of which it fixes in advance.

The followers of Descartes more and more will free human speech from a resemblance to any kind of divine language. Mathematics is certainly the language in which the universe is written, as Galileo said, but that language is the work of man, the fruit of conquest. Already, the wisdom of a Descartes who sees himself as master and possessor of nature is the wisdom of the workman, the technician, conscious of an increasing freedom of action. It's no longer a matter of divining the plan of God, or of reading it over His shoulder, but of taking the initiative, adding to nature. Man makes himself creator, in the image of God—or if need be without Him. This humanism shows a greater and greater interest in the activity of the mind. An intellectualist reasoning is substituted for the ontological reasoning of traditional philosophy. Judgment by-passes concept and idea along that road which leads through the 18th century from Descartes to Kant.

The thinker of the 18th century, a contemporary of the industrial revolution and a precursor of the political revolution of 1789, ascribes more and more efficacy to man. Science and technology steal primacy in this world from God. The *Encyclopedia* sets forth on a human scale the inventory of the new universe. The concept of language also expresses this inflexibility of philosophy. The century of systems gives to thought the power of sustaining the universe. But the reform must be radical. It is necessary to wipe the tablet clean of all the accumulated misunderstandings of those unfortunate ages deprived of enlightenment, by taking up once more the very project Descartes had laid out in his letter to Mersenne. "The words we have scarcely have anything but confused meanings . . ."; all error comes from that source Locke, Berkeley, and Condillac will repeat after Descartes. Each in his own way will condemn the ills of established language in the traditional doctrines of metaphysics. The young Descartes had retreated before the enterprise which had seemed to him utopian. His successors will be more intrepid: the power which the theologians had recognized as God's to designate reality while creating it henceforth belongs to the philosopher who, by drawing up a rigorous inventory of thoughts without theological prejudice, becomes the real creator of the world of reason. The revolution on the linguistic level begins then on the night of the 4th of August when all traditional privileges are abolished. It ends with a new constitution which, under the authority of sovereign reason, maintains the free play of words, citizens of the universe of discourse, the meanings of which have previously been carefully verified. Just as for the revolutionaries of 1789 a good political structure must assure the happiness of man, so too the ideologues, revolutionaries of philosophy, think with Condillac that a "well-made language" will forever solve all problems.

The political Revolution is solidified by a defeat. It had announced peace to the world, and instead declared war on it. It had promised civic concord; it ended in the Terror. The 19th century, after the Napoleonic flood-tide, was a century of reaction, of return to traditional values. Linguistics reflects in its own way this disaster for the current optimisms. Condillac dies without having been able to elaborate that *Langue des Calculs* which was to put an end to philosophy by a systematic completeness. By a curious contradiction of history, a science of language begins to constitute itself from then on. But this science, contrary to any analogy and all mathematical formalism, is a science of man. To the 18th century, the century of philosophers, is opposed the 19th century, the century of philologists. A language cannot be reduced to an artificial system, to a symbolization of reason. During the romantic age, it appears as the incarnation in words of the genius of a people. The established language, the confusion of which Descartes and his successors had condemned, represents in reality a kind of communal examination of conscience, a cultural horizon pervading each personal thought. A new ontology is sketched out here, following the works of Humboldt, Jacob Grimm, and the German scholars. It is an ontology for which Renan will be the spokesman in France, an ontology no longer founded on divine reason or the activity of the mind, but on national values. A language constitutes an organic whole developing through history as a living being. It constitutes in each age a sort of collective unconscious, upon which are nourished the enchanted speech of poets as well as the folktales of the story-tellers and popular wisdom.

The romantic age thus elaborates a mythology of language, rediscovering that the Greek word *mythos* means in point of fact *speech*. The works of the comparative linguists, the discoveries of etymology, the identification of an Indo-European family of languages will all serve as fanciful pretexts for the hypotheses of the most radical theoreticians of nationalism whose claims suffocate the age of enlightenment's dream of rational universality. Man is now only the servant of collective bodies whose languages attest to their endurance. Unfortunately, there is a link between German philosophy of the 19th century and the myth of the 20th century according to the nationalsocialist ideologues. They invoked the spirit of the race, rediscovered in language and archaic institutions, in order to justify the most monstrous aspects of a regime that, for a moment, held Europe at its mercy.

The defeat of Nazism is thus in a certain sense the defeat of a philosophy of language. Unfortunately, our age hardly seems capable of perfecting the unitary language that would serve as the common standard, in good will, for the peoples of the world who are more and more united by the very development of civilization. The United Nations organization has run foul of the same difficulties as once did the League of Nations. The clash of idioms, the clash of values perpetuates upon humanity the curse of Babel.

The meaning of human speech, then, remains unresolved. All the metaphysics proposed over the centuries seem to end up in failure. Human language is not the Word of God the creator, and cannot claim to repeat that Word. Nor is it any longer the artificial work of an intellect free to elaborate a symbolic language in terms of the norms of rational intelligibility alone. The successes of science must not delude us in this respect, for they are limited to those areas circumscribing or reigning within a non-human objective reality. Finally, human speech is not subjugated to a system of social phenomena that would enclose it in the concentration camp of the collective unconscious. Speech does not keep us in bondage to being, and it does not permit us complete license. Speech is neither being nor the absence of being, but an engagement of the person in things and others. Putting it another way, reflection on language ought not to begin with God, reason, or society, but with human reality, which finds in speech a mode of self-affirmation and establishment in the world. The problem is not a problem of language *per se*, but a problem of speaking man.

IV / Speaking as Human Reality

THUS, language does not constitute an exemplary reality, detached from speaking men, a divine Word, a closed and perfect system, a spiritual mechanism disciplining personal lives by its ontological force. Man's speech is not content merely to reflect an antecedent reality. Such would take away from it all intrinsic efficacy. Any philosophy for which man is not the basic measure divides speech into a transcendent creating language and a created human language deprived of all initiative and reality. Even adding these two languages together is not equivalent to human speech.

Henceforth, we must consider speech not as an objective system, in the third person, but as an individual enterprise: to begin speaking is one of the major tasks of man. This formula must be clarified word by word; language does not exist before that personal initiative which brings it into being. The established language offers only an outline for the full development of verbal activity. Words and their meanings embody end-

[35]

less and constantly changing possibilities which are offered the man who speaks. Personal language, in reality, is not enslaved to the dictionary. Rather, it is the dictionary which carries the burden of reflecting language in action, and of cataloguing its meanings.

A living language, therefore, appears as the language of living men. At the very heart of the community the vocabulary of each individual changes with time. There is a history of language peculiar to each great writer—but as well and more modestly, one could pick out variations of speech for every man throughout the development of his life. And so too, changes are not limited to vocabulary alone, for a language is not a collection of words. Linguists have shown that the basic unit of living speech is not in the form of nouns, verbs, or adjectives, all isolated from one another like so many grains in a sack. The unit of speech is a complex whole, given vitality by the intended meaning of the speaker: it is the *verbal image* that is expressed in more or less complex sentences, sometimes reduced to a single word, but always corresponding to the expression of a meaning. One must not think that within the experience of consciousness a sentence is constructed merely from words. It's much truer to say that words are the sedimentary deposits of sentences in which the desires of expression are manifested.

Nothing can better show the fact that human speech is always an act. Authentic language intervenes in a given situation as a moment of that situation or as a reaction to that situation. Its function is to maintain or re-establish a balance, to assure the insertion of the person in the world, to achieve communication. Now, situations continually recur in the course of personal biography without ever reproducing themselves exactly—to such a degree that the meaning of a word, far from being fixed once and for all, is novel in each of its re-embodiments. The dictionary only presents a list of average and so to speak statistical values. "The word," Henry Delacroix said, "is created each time that it is uttered." [1]

Thus we rediscover the creative character of speaking in action. This fact has been recognized, in their own manner, by primitive peoples and by theologians, who make the Word an attribute of divinity. Language illustrates the transcendence of human reality, alone capable of constituting the world. Before speech, the world is merely the present and continually disappearing context of human activities, a context in which even the limits between personality and environment are not clearly defined. Language supplies denomination, precision, decision; both awareness and knowledge. The name creates the object; it alone reaches it beyond the inconstancy of appearances. But as well it creates personal existence. To objects in the world correspond states of mind, the mere designation of which provides the resolution of internal ambiguities. To say to oneself: "I am sick," or "I am in love," "I am shy," or "I am stingy" is to find the solution of the riddle, to give a solution to the riddle of personal uncertainties, and thereby to go beyond uncertainty. The use of language creates for us beyond the present an enduring nature fit to explain the past and determine the future.

Speaking constitutes the essence of the world and the essence of man. Each sentence orients us in a world which, moreover, is not given as such, once and for all, but appears to be constructed word by word. Even the most insignificant expression contributes to this work

1. *Societé Francaise de Philosophie,* December 14, 1922.

of continuous reconstruction. Just as each word mastered by the young child increases his universe, so too for the adult the act of speaking continually contributes to existence. Traditional theories are wrong in seeing in language a kind of mental duplication of the world—as if the universe of discourse could exist outside of the universe of things, as if words were not all that we can grasp of the world, its intrinsic reality and the flesh of its flesh. The world is given to each of us as a body of meanings, the disclosure of which we obtain only on the level of speech. Language is reality. As Sartre has picturesquely put it, "from within, man keeps oozing like cheeze; he is not. . . ." In order to stop this "monotonous hemorrhage," man must accept self-determination, self-definition, in other words take on a certain number of designations which give him his nationality, his profession, his social class, in brief his "situation" in the world of words, which is the world of values and of beings. For lack of this, all that remains of him "is a little bit of dirty water gurgling down the drain." [2]

To name is to call into existence, to draw out from nothingness. That which is not named cannot exist in any possible way. Even the God of the Old Testament who refuses to state his name must accept being represented in the universe of human speech by the word "Yahweh." Nietzsche very rightly said that men of genius are ordinarily "namers." Genius consists in "seeing something which does not yet bear a name although the whole world has it in view." [3] Newton creates gravity, Bergson intuition, Kant creates transcendental consciousness as Einstein creates relativity, and as the modern physicists have created electricity. . . .

2. *Situations*, N.R.F., 1947, p. 218.
3. Nietzsche, *The Gay Science*, #261.

Naming establishes a right to existence. It is words that make things and beings, that define the relations according to which the order of the world is constituted. To situate oneself in the world, for each of us, is to be at peace with the network of words that put everything in its place in the environment. Our *lived space* is a space of speaking, a pacified territory in which each name is a solution to a problem. Human relations themselves appear as a vast system of words which one gives and receives according to rhythms established by social class and manners. The social order is defined by a code of correct denominations wherein all disagreement, all difference immediately appears as a sign of disharmony. If my wife, my children, my friends, my students, my superiors, or my inferiors no longer address me by the names I rightfully expect of each of them, a certain anxiety arises: revolution threatens—or mental disintegration. Anxiety about language always accompanies the alienation of man, rupture with the world, and it demands a return to order or the establishment of a new order. To put words in order is to put thoughts in order and to put men in order. Each one of us, insofar as he is a member of a family, a supporter of a party, a member of a professional body, or a citizen of a nation and of the international community, finds himself engaged in that task of assuring the correctness of names, of which the Emperors of China were already so well aware.

For each of us language accompanies the creation of the world—it is the agent of that creation. It is by speaking that man comes into the world and the world comes into thought. Speaking manifests the being of the world, the being of man, and the being of thought. All spoken words, even in negative or self-deceptive speech, attest to the horizons of thought and the world. The creation of the world is the creation of man, the call to be human. Language puts things in perspective according to their meaning. That's why it presents to us not a physics, but more specifically a *meta-physics* of reality; it always presupposes beyond its apparent and material tenor an integration as a function of total human reality. The intuition of value orients and justifies the affirmation of existence by the invocation of a transcendent reality generative of any ontology. Language is given to us as the currency of inexpressible being. It is backed by things, man, and God, and is the sign of an encounter and reciprocal fidelity of the real and the true in human consciousness.

Unfortunately, that apotheosis of language immediately casts itself in doubt. If words command access to being, if it is true that before and beyond words there is nothing, how is it that the word often appears suspect and devalued? It is the currency of being, in theory, but all too often counterfeit. The idea of an ontology of language thus immediately runs up against the objection of *error,* an objection that obviously only makes sense if speech is in intention the bearer of truth. In fact, the life of mind ordinarily begins not with the acquisition of language, but with revolt against language once it is acquired. The child discovers the world through the established language, which those around prescribe for him. The adolescent discovers values in the *revolt* against the language he had until then blindly trusted and which seems to him, in the light of the crisis, destitute of all authenticity. Every man worthy of the name has known that crisis in the appreciation of language which causes one to pass from naive confidence to doubt and denial. "Freedom," exclaims the disappointed revolutionary, "freedom, what crimes are committed in thy name?" "Nature," declares the repentant romantic, "with this word one has lost all." "Virtue, thou art only a name," Brutus proclaims in defeat before he kills himself. Hamlet, the very hero of the lucidity of despair, gives the ultimate formula of all these disenchantments with language: "Words! words! words!"

The radical revolt of Hamlet inevitably leads him to death. To disavow language is to lose the sense of reality. The Prince of Denmark, at the moment of his death, will only say: "the rest is silence," the last meaningful speech of that renunciation of the universe of discourse which is equivalent to a renunciation of being. This linguistic denial, moreover, is often held in a less extreme form; it is usually expressed as a moment in the realization of a new being in the world. That moment of criticism and of self-awareness, that moment of a new departure of thought and action, is the moment of the ironic questioner Socrates who demands from his victim the meaning of this or that everyday word. Without seeing the trap laid by the jovial sphinx, he replies by giving the accepted definition. But Socrates has no trouble at all in showing the insufficiency of the notion he proposes. He forces his victim into self-contradiction and, by a skillful polemical maneuver, he proposes to lead him from discord to reconciliation, from the illusion of common sense to the correctness of good sense.

The Socratic parable allows the testing of language to be given its due. The established language sanctifies an agreed-upon meaning which initially gains our uncritical adherence. The words of everyday language belong to everyone and no one, stripped of all actuality

—that is to say, of all value. Words, as we have seen, have had their origin in the mutual engagement of man and the world; but they tend to free themselves from their immediate context. Although a word is the *meaning* of the situation and although it is a kind of promise of that situation, even if not explicit, it has a value independent of the situation, making possible a great economy of action. At the same time, speech, which is human reality, masks the absence of that reality. It is a reality by default. There is truth only at the level of speech, but error is contemporaneous with truth. A goodly number of words that we pronounce in the course of the day are false, attestations of a sympathy, a cordiality, or an interest that we do not feel—as the recriminations of the misanthrope illustrate.

By being witness to the authenticity of being, language is also its counterfeit. The common meanings blunt the proper meanings of each word. The words of each person become the words of everyone only by losing their intention, by being progressively degraded, as new and shiny money once put into circulation grows dull. Instead of coinciding with value, the word is now only its label. It avoids the subtlety of a more direct expression; *sunt verba et voces*, said the Latin poet, *praetereaque nihil*—words and formulas and nothing else. Thus the sedimentation of being into having becomes possible, that decline which empties speaking of its substance and efficacy, thereby making any revolt justifiable. Because he who takes language as coin of the realm is carried by speech toward non-existent values, he will be the dupe of whoever manipulates him, and his good faith having been seduced, he will now only see bad faith all about him.

Further, the usurpation of language does not merely

involve the social degradation of words, nor the abuse of our listener's confidence. More profoundly, language inserts itself into the self-consciousness of each man as a screen that distorts him in his own eyes. The intimate being of man is in fact confused, indistinct, and multiple. Language intervenes as a power destined to expropriate us from ourselves in order to bring us into line with those around, in order to model us to the common measure of all. It defines and perfects us, it terminates and determines us. The control of consciousness it exercises makes it the accomplice of having, in its monolithic poverty, as opposed to the plurality of being. To the degree that we are forced to resort to language we renounce our interior life because language imposes the discipline of exteriority. The use of speech is thus one of the essential causes of the unhappy conscience, all the more essential because we cannot be without it. It is this which Bruce Parain has strongly emphasized:

> "At every moment, each consciousness destroys a little bit of the vocabulary it has received and against which it cannot fail to revolt, because it is not its; but immediately it recreates another vocabulary in which it once again disappears."

That's why the human condition seems to the writer a "condition of generalized revolt and suicide." [4]

The spiritedness of this reaction reveals a beautiful if however somewhat naive soul. It is true that language presupposes a certain number of sedimented values in the surrounding culture, which remain at the fossile stage as long as they remain purely external assumptions. The trouble is authentic value is not a

4. "Le Language et L'existence," in the collection: *L'existence*, N.R.F., 1945, p. 165.

thing: awareness crystallized into common meanings possesses no real right to impose a direction upon consciousness. Every affirmation of value implies a personal initiative, and a kind of recovery of the elements of language by an awareness which rediscovers them and which alone is able to attest to their authenticity. Whoever is duped here is first of all duped by himself: he has not yet attained his spiritual maturity. Crisis is a sign of graduation to manhood. It is resolved when the person succeeds in finding within himself a more solid foundation than the shifting sands of the common language.

To toss recriminations against language is to be the dupe of language, wrongfully to attribute to it a capacity it does not possess. And the very revolt is perhaps not exempt from self-deception (*mauvaise foi*). To condemn language is ordinarily to protest against others, to condemn those others considered responsible for this established perversion. Now the blame is always shared: the man who does the blaming is not blameless insofar as he does so. It is not only others who *break their word,* but most of all he who entered with others into a community founded upon a misconception, the collective work of all those who participate in it. Thus, rather than indicting others and their word, it is better to pass from revolt to conversion. It is better to pass to a decisive and positive affirmation of oneself.

Putting it in a different way, language cannot justify anything and everything. It is up to each person to assume the responsibility for his own language by searching for the *right word.* In the place of an objective or sociological ontology of speech a personal ontology must be substituted. Discourse is merely an affirmation of being which it behooves each to make authentic. Words do not lie, but man does. I do not fulfill the business of being with words, but only with myself, and with my own fidelity. The infantile conception of a magical efficacy of speech in itself gives way to that more difficult conception that language is for man a privileged means of carving out for himself a road across material and moral obstacles in order to reach being—that is to say the decisive values worthy of orienting his destiny.

Thus human speech is not subordinate to a determinism that in advance would distort it in the direction of a transcendent finality, the divine Word, or collective consciousness. The only finality is an immanent finality, the necessity of assuring in the total behavior of man the coincidence of being and doing. A dead language invokes absent and long-dead values. Living speech acknowledges the requirement of the spiritual life in travail—not at all a closed system achieved once and for all—but an effort of constant regeneration. For an entire people as well as for a writer, a fixed tongue is a sign of decay. Likewise, there is no *last word* in personal affirmation before the last moment of existence itself. In that pursuit of being appears the essence of language. It is strictly bound up with the very essence of man, which it has the task of revealing to the world—an impossibly rigorous and yet necessary task. The ultimate sense of speaking is of the moral order. Only an ethic can unite the various means of approaching the activity of speaking. Speech, in its full reality, manifests the transcendent power of man who, by inserting himself in the world, gives meaning to himself and to the world. It is this major task in which each personality manifests what it is capable of: its creative power or its inability to pass from mental confusion to human reality, from the chaos of impressions, things, and values to the fundamental unity of mature affirmation.

.

V / Speaking as Encounter

MAN CALLS THE WORLD into being. One might add, as well, that the world calls man, that it waits for the revelation of man in order to be fully expressed. But this reciprocity of man and world does not in itself constitute the original situation from which language emerges. Man speaks the world, but he doesn't speak *to* the world, or if he does it is because the world has assumed for him the new form of an *alter ego*. It has been personified in order to become the other, the opposite participant in the dialogue—for example, Nature as invoked by the poet.

Thus the understanding of language must not be limited to those two opposing terms, self and world. A third term is called for, the *other* to whom my speech is directed. I speak because I am not alone. Even in a soliloquy, in speaking to myself, I refer to myself as an other, I communicate from myself to myself. Language, from its most rudimentary form onward, testifies to a movement of personal being outside of itself. The infant when he smiles and, all too quickly, when he cries is appealing to those around, from whom he expects a response. Human being is not contained within itself. The contours of one's body outline a line of demarcation, but never an absolute limit. The existence of others doesn't appear as the delayed result of experience and reason. Intellectually and materially, the other is for each man a condition of existence. The plurality of individuals, the fragmentation of being, appears thus as an original presupposition of lived consciousness. The primitive, in the initial stages of human evolution, does not think of himself as an autonomous person. He apprehends himself in participation, engaged in the larger vital rhythms of the tribe—not one over against all, but one with all.

In essence, language is not of one but of many; it is *between*. It expresses the relational being of man. The sensory-motor organs anticipate the schema of a universe upon which all behavior will depend, just as the psycho-biological phenomenon foreordains a communal destiny. As it is progressively elaborated, language from here on consolidates and multiplies communication. Through communication it makes a new world, the real world.

Thus a new situation is established: the view that the creative initiative of a self takes possession of the universe becomes dubious. The self does not by itself alone have to carve out for itself an access to being—because the self exists only in reciprocity with the other. An isolated self can truly be said to be only an abstraction. Putting it another way, no man ever invented language *ab ovo*. It is undoubtedly because this was somehow obscurely felt that the wisdom of the ages reserved to God the privilege of that creation. All language is initially received; the infant receives it ready-made from his environment, as he receives his nourishment. No matter how far back we go in history the root origin of language escapes us. Words are there even before the emergence of personal awareness, to which they propose or on which they impose crystallized meanings. It is through words that meanings will be sought, through the mediation of words, like a kind of substance which one must learn how to mould in order to use.

Before speech there has always been a tongue, before the language-subject a language-object. It is a determinate reality, constituted by others, and the learning of it is imposed upon the child by others. Language here is a world, or rather it is the world that must be discovered word by word in passing from babbling, that "verbal scribbling" as Henri Delacroix called it, to articulated speech. From primitive mental confusion, objects and values will be little by little disengaged and designated by the authority of adults. His very existence, moreover, will be taught to the child in this indirect way. It will take a long time for him to situate himself as an object in a world of objects and it is on the model of the other that he will become conscious of his personal reality. He speaks of himself in the third person before attaining the first person.

From the very beginning, language marks out the point of encounter between the self and others. For a long time it will sanctify the dependence of the self on others, since, before beginning to speak, one must have received speech ready-made. Moreover, the struggle for domination between a common meaning and personal initiative will never cease. It defines the limits of human speech. If I speak it is less for myself than for the other; I speak in order to address myself to the other, in order to make myself understood. Here, speaking is like a *hyphen*. But for the other to understand me, my language must be his—it must give precedence to the other over me. It is all the more intelligible the more it is a common denominator. Others have taught me to speak, have given me speech. But in doing this, they have perhaps suffocated an original voice in me, a voice both weak and slow to free itself. To say that language is other people is tantamount to saying that we are from childhood on reduced to captivity by our forced submission to the ready-made formulas of the established language. By a kind of paradoxical inversion, the individual finds himself deprived of the benefit of that magnificent invention of speech, an invention that, as we have seen, established the sovereignty of human space. Seemingly, it is the invention of everyone but of no one in particular—an invention that, for each of us, amounts to a falling in step, a forced alignment with others, in other words a definitive alienation.

Thus is formulated a fundamental antinomy of human speech, the self-affirmation of the subject at the same time as the search for others. On the one hand, we have the expressive function of language: I speak in order to make myself understood, in order to emerge into reality, in order to add myself to nature. On the other hand, we have the communicative function: I speak in order to reach out to others, and I can join myself to them all the more insofar as I set aside what is mine alone. This polarity of expression and communication corresponds to the opposition between the first person and the third, between individual subjectivity and the objectivity of meaning held in common. That duality seems to tear in half the activity of human speech and to symbolize its failure since it would seem

that speech can never simultaneously fulfill both its
centripetal and centrifugal functions. Can it say everything to everyone?

Many thinkers have taken one or the other side of
the split and have thus admitted more or less clearly
that expression and communication vary in inverse
proportions to one another. If I want to be understood by
all, I ought to use the language of everyone else, and
therefore renounce in me whatever makes me different
from everybody. Such is the meaning of *"basic"* French,
a language of a few hundred words, constituted by statistical research and supposedly capable of making any
foreigner readily understood by any Frenchman. The
most common language represents a universal password. And so the most obscure writer gives up his
refinements of vocabulary and style when he speaks to
the corner grocer or the bus driver. When Mallarmé
wrote delicate quatrains on envelopes in the place of
addresses, he counted on the particular good will of the
employees of the postal service to decipher these poetic
conundrums. But if all the users of the postal service
had done the same thing it is probable that this service
would soon have ceased to function. Carried to the
extreme, if I use an entirely personal language, one
completely fabricated by me—like Panurge in the three
of the fourteen languages that he uses successively in
his first encounter with Pantagruel—it is clear that I
shall succeed thereby in expressing radically original
formulas, but that no one will understand me. Such is
the case with certain mental illnesses in which words,
foreign to the prevailing linguistic usage, only have
meaning for the one who expresses them. Likewise, the
Hindu brahman, when he pronounces the mystic syl-

lable *Om,* in which is summed up for him the very presence of being, says everything and at the same time says nothing.

It seems then that the use of speech obliges us to choose between two opposite forms of alienation. On the one hand, like the madman or the mystic, we can speak as no one else speaks. On the other hand, like the practitioner of a "basic" language, we can speak as everyone else does. In both cases the very meaning of personality is done away with. The more I communicate, the less I express myself; the more I express myself, the less I communicate. It is necessary to choose between incomprehensibility and inauthenticity—between excommunication and self-denial.

The dilemma is not arbitrary. Many eminent philosophers have declared themselves for one side or the other. The thought of Bergson, for example, puts in opposition the superficial self, contaminated by language which makes it a thing among other things, and the profound self, an inexpressible incantation, the authenticity of a thought resisting all formulation, a mystical effusion, a pure poetry. Communication kills expression. Salvation consists in a kind of reconversion. One must renounce language, break away from existence geometrized by common meaning, in order to identify with the meaning of vital inspiration within oneself. Such is the basic faithfulness of the hero and the saint. Over against Bergsonian intuition, founded as it is upon the condemnation of the established language, Durkheim affirms the authority of common meaning as it is formalized within various collective phenomena. Durkheim revives Auguste Comte's declaration that there is no autonomous psychological reality. Man is a biological being who receives his entire education from society. The individual is only an abstraction, destitute of all positive existence. The community causes us to be: with language and in language it gives us concepts and moral rules. Our duty then is to submit without reservation, to adhere strictly to this social control over the individual consciousness. Turning inward and the expressive intention seem to be temptations that ought to be banished, temptations that lead down the road of error and crime.

The opposition of Bergson and Durkheim is reflected in other thinkers as well. Charles Blondel, the student of both these masters, strove to reconcile these two doctrines by identifying the pure self of Bergson with the morbid personality of the schizophrenic, whose alienation specifically consists in just that rapture of the social pact of language. Speaking depersonalizes us, or rather reifies us, but for our own good. On the other hand, such intellectualist philosophers as Brunschvicg and Alain likewise saw language as the salutary instrument of the preponderance of exteriority over interiority, but thanks now to the providential intervention of Reason and no longer Society. Man at the mercy of himself, and attempting to express the vicissitudes of his own intimate being—a Maine de Biran, an Amiel, even a Montaigne—finally patterns himself on the rhythms of his own cenesthesia. His song expresses nothing more than the state of his own viscera. Maturity is not found in this monologue of the humors. True maturity requires that the person abandon all self-satisfaction and throw himself into his work in order to bring his contribution to the common structure of objective wisdom, the model for which is given us by the rationality and universality of science. Language appears here as prime cause. It brings with it a control of consciousness that makes us reasonable if we know how to obey it—that is to say if we know how to develop the invitation which it brings to us to emerge from confusion and inner chaos in order to produce according to intelligible norms.

These various doctrines bring into the closed field of language a dispute which jeopardizes the entire destiny of man. According to them, one must choose between interiority and exteriority, between expression and communication. It is precisely this obligation to choose, to slice in two, which seems a principle of error in so far as it leads thinkers into failing to take into account the specific nature of the human person. The individual finds himself divided and parcelled-out under different headings: the biological self of *élan vital,* the social self, the rational self. We are asked to commit ourselves in favor of one of these aspects to the exclusion of the others, whichever of them is held to be most valuable (no passing from one to the other allowed). Because of this, in spite of all attempts to conceal it, the neglected aspect always makes its influence felt as the intellectualist's bad conscience about the vital, the vitalist's about the intellectualist, and the sociologist's about the individual aspects all indicate. Nevertheless, in principle human unity and identity is given initially: man is at once the collective consciousness, reason, and the pure self who refuses society and reason.

Each man is all of these together. The concrete person achieves a balance for himself between these various aspects. Speaking formulates that balance in the process of achievement, at one and the same time expression of pure self and participation in the social and the rational. From this point of view the opposition established between the self and the other seems completely inadequate. Besides, it repeats the common individualist complaint against mass tyranny. Others prevent me from being myself, they act as an obstacle to the full realization of what I am—so the anarchist maintains, a Max Stirner for example. The community is the prison in which *they* imprison the *I*. That is why I cannot be myself and be content unless I rely on myself. Hence the theme of the literary or philosophic ivory tower. It is a citadel in which a person, in order fully to affirm himself, brackets the whole of humanity and devotes himself in solitude to the search for true expression.

It is all too easy to show the error of this black and white dichotomy. Cut off in his tower in Perigord, Montaigne was not alone, because his tower was a library— and the search for self in which he delighted was intended as well for others. "No pleasure has any savor for me without communication. Not even a merry thought comes to my mind without my being vexed at having produced it alone without anyone to offer it to." [1] Descartes, before the fire, separated himself only the better to be united to the entirety of humanity. Vigny, another solitary, will toss the bottle into the sea from his tower, Maine-Giraud, as an appeal for the confidant worthy of him. The sickly Proust closes himself up in his soundproof room. And yet, he himself said of Noah that he was never more present to the world than in the ark, although the ark was closed and darkness covered the earth. Finally, Stirner, the complete anarchist, writes a book to protest, in the name of the individual, against the masses; but the very publication of his book indicates an attempt to convert the masses. . . . If the writer or the thinker withdraws, it is not in order to be alone. The withdrawal is not an absence, but rather the

1. Montaigne, *Essays*, III, 9.

pursuit of a real presence. The attack on inauthentic communication is only the negative aspect, the other side of the coin of the anguished striving for authenticity.

It's not a question, then, of an inverse relation between expression and communication. The two intentions of human speech are complimentary. Pure expression, detached from all communication, remains a fiction, because all speech implies aiming toward others. To break silence, if only with a cry of anguish or a song without words, is still to address someone, to call to witness, to call for help. The social pact of communication is never broken except to produce better communication. The anarchist himself here refuses obedience only in order to affirm the necessity of a truer obedience. In other words, the denial of communication as a fact implies the nostalgia for communication as a value. When surrealism, in its search for pure expression, denied all discipline of thought and uttered words in their primitive state, it still dreamed of inventing a newer and more vivid language. The proof of this, moreover, lies in the fact that there was a surrealistic reading public and a coterie of surrealists communicating in the affirmation of certain values. Every expression seeks to obtain the *recognition* of other people. I want to be known as I am, in my basic sincerity, to men and to God himself. I expect this recognition as a confirmation of my being and as a contribution to my being.

Inversely, the idea of a communication without expression is senseless, because my language can never be absolutely expropriated. It would not exist unless a personal intention had initially brought it into being. If I speak, it is because I have something to say; an *I* is always necessary as the subject of a phrase. If my language consisted of "speaking like everyone else," if it merely repeated what someone else said, still it would mean that I rally myself to the common opinion, an act that presupposes a self-commitment I might always have refused. Even if, in the interests of objectivity, I suppress myself in order to leave speech in the hands of others, it would still remain true that the *We* is an assemblage of *I*'s. There is no social contract without common consent. Every act of speech thus has a personal function corresponding to that initiative which situates us in language and posits us in placing us over against one another.

Thus, one must admit the existence of an intimate union between communication and expression. In fact, authentic communication is not simply the exchange of devalued words in which no one is involved. Chatter and passing the time of day represent not the highest attainment, but a caricature of communion between men. True communication is the realization of a unity, i.e. a piece of common labor. It is the unity of each with the other, but at the same time the unifying of each with himself, the rearrangement of personal life in the encounter with others. I cannot communicate as long as I do not try to bring to the other the profound sense of my being. The communion of love, which represents one of the most complete modes of understanding between two persons, can't be achieved without a recall of personality, each discovering himself in the contact with the other. Every real relation is communication by persons and not simply by things; more specifically, things enter in only as symbols of persons. The purest expression, the affirmation of spirit in art, founds a new communion, and perfect communication liberates in us possibilities of expression that until then lay dormant.

The fundamental error here is in holding to a conception that reduces language to words, an insipid conception according to which a word is a word, a meaning is a meaning. In reality, a tongue isn't merely a kind of pre-established mechanism to which one purely and simply joins himself. A tongue only exists as a necessary condition for the act of speaking. It has to be recovered and realized by that effort of expression thanks to which the person establishes himself as a function of verbal reality. An impersonal "basic" language represents the lowest degree of intention and expression. Just as the established tongue is only the terrain for speech, so too speech appears as the necessary means of communication that fixes the moment in which speaking establishes a new language, the moment in which the *we* is realized in the union of *I* and *you*.

The manly task of beginning to speak demands of us then that we pass from the materiality of words to their value-meaning. Our concrete freedom is established to the extent of our capacity to foster at one and the same time expression and communication within the language that makes us manifest. And once this principle is admitted, one must give up the dream of an absolute freedom, a freedom limited, perhaps, to the God who has created all things by naming them. Neither in metaphysics nor in politics does man enjoy such radical initiative—his freedom is a conditioned freedom, a situational freedom which begins by obedience, that is to say by the recognition of what is. To be free is to give a form, but whether we like it or not we must accept the fact that a foundation is first given to us. The nihilist of language, the surrealist, who atomizes human speech simply for the pleasure of destroying it, and who is incapable of any discipline whatever, thereby indicates that he is far less free than the great writer who creates an original style with the words common to everyone. The highest freedom begins communally— no longer a freedom that separates, but a freedom that unites.

VI / Communication

IN CONTRAST to the impersonality of dead third-person language, expression manifests the *I*. Communication is a search for the *you* and the *I* and the *you* tend to join together in the unity of *we*. All of this testifies to living language. It remains for us to specify the meaning of these two aspects of a single enterprise.

At the beginning, the situation is given by the established tongue, the common stuff of every exchange of speech. A tongue is a social phenomenon which sums up within itself the institutions of a national community. It sets up a balance at the same time that it fixes norms. "There is as it were a tacit agreement," wrote the eminent linguist Vendryes, "established as a matter of course between the individuals of the same group to maintain the tongue as the rules prescribe." [1] The linguistic "contract" is one of the fundamental aspects of the social contract. The will to live together, constitutive of a nation, is established through the preservation

1. Vendryes, *Le Langage*, Renaissance du Livre, 1921, p. 283.

of a common inheritance of understanding. Under the cloak of words, a tongue is the symbol of a communion in value. The claim to nationality has always been associated in history with the defense of a tongue, and that has at times been carried as far as the more or less artificial resurrection of a defunct idiom, as we can see in the case of Ireland or the state of Israel.

But the established language must not be understood as a closed system. A living tongue appears to be animated by a mysterious movement, as if the collective agreement that sustains it were in a state of constant renewal. Every attempt authoritatively to fix a tongue at any given moment in its evolution is doomed to failure, as witness the experience of the French Academy, charged by Richelieu, who was trying to establish absolute monarchy, to infuse order into the language. Now the dictionary, the standard of good usage, finds itself incapable of fixing that usage. Here, the royal will is powerless: a dictionary catalogues the state of a tongue at any given moment. It cannot halt its accounting. As soon as it reaches the end, it must start all over again, pursuing from edition to edition that ideal which it will never reach until France has ceased to exist. A tongue, then, is not a compendium, but a moving horizon. And its total evolution is only a mass of individual contributions which day by day elaborate the spoken reality.

And so, if it is true to say that the tongue furnishes the framework for the exercise of speech, one must recognize as well that the tongue only exists within the act of speaking which assumes it and fosters it. The established language defines a *field of comprehension*. Communication is the relation of two subjects situated in this field, a field that furnishes them a common domain of reference, a background against which their momentary relation stands out as a figure. But this *cultural horizon* doesn't exhaust the conditions for communication. It is itself as it were enveloped in an *anthropological horizon* of which it appears as a particular determination. Before speaking any particular tongue, man speaks, man is a relational being, and that relational nature of human reality is the most general condition for any spoken exchange. The human relation in general conditions the cultural relation, and the latter, in its turn, conditions the entry into relation of several personalities, whose encounter assumes a character of more or less intimacy according to the nature of the interests that motivate it.

The human horizon, the cultural horizon, and the personal horizon, fitted the one into the other, constitute the field of comprehension as the common moment of the two histories that meet. The landscape of communication, then, is not given once and for all in a massive simplicity. It is itself made up of a series of successive backgrounds against which the present reality of the conversation stands out. Action reacts against backdrop and recreates it; the reciprocity of the beings present to one another is projected as a new environment expressing the state of relations at each moment of their history. That's the reason for the extreme complexity of those aspects of communication which are never made completely explicit. The simplest relation opens up endless vistas, and its beginning, like its end, often appears difficult to determine strictly. For communication always presupposes previous communication, but it produces a new communication which will persist even though the relation be ended. The balance at the beginning is destroyed by the intention to communicate, which leads to the realization of a new balance.

Let us suppose that I am walking in the streets of a foreign city in which I do not know the native tongue. I feel like Ovid, exiled to the edge of the Black sea: *barbarus hic ego sum, quia non Intelligor ulli:* incapable of making myself understood, I am the barbarian, the Latin poet said sadly. However, he was one who felt himself representative of a much higher civilization among those backward peoples. Etymologically, for the Greeks, the *barbarian* is the man who stammers an inarticulate language and who is scorned for his poor elocution. Overcoming this self-conscious state of the foreigner who feels ridiculous, I accost a passer-by in order to ask him for information. In spite of the difference of tongues, the sense of human solidarity creates between him and me the possibility of a relation. Now this man recognizes my nationality and speaks to me in my own tongue. Between us is established the solidarity of a culture, the respect for certain values. A true understanding will be born in this encounter. I am henceforth bound in reciprocity with my host for all time to come. And through this representative, the country itself where I have been well received will profit from my sympathy.

It is thus that the relation of communication is established, as the mutual contact of two subjects whose meeting determines a field of reference against which a common form comes to be realized. A relation is not possible outside of the recognition of an authority, outside of an *invocation*, that is to say a shared obedience which assures the unity, short-lived or profound, of

persons encountering one another. Mutual understanding, then, appears in each instance as a commitment. I
risk myself in confiding myself to others, as others risk
themselves to me, in the guise of the words we
exchange. Undoubtedly, the rules of social life and good
manners intervene to limit the risks. Each of us strives
to protect his privacy against the encroachments of
others. Be that as it may, and in spite of these safe-
guards, every encounter is an adventure that can lead us
far, because, in the beautiful words of the Austrian poet
Hugo von Hofmannstahl, "each encounter disintegrates
us and reintegrates us. . . ."

Each act of speaking must be grasped in context
according to the being it invokes. The most obvious
material meaning, the literal text of the message, hides
a formal meaning. Words announce an intention. They
seek to convert. Confident of the previous adherence,
which I have discerned in others, to certain values that
exist as a common denominator for us, I try to enlarge
or deepen this common consent. To the peculiar efficacy
of words is added the magic of presence as an extra
charge to gain conviction. The least and most banal
word is elevated by the power of enchantment that
envelops it. The order of words realizes to a certain
extent the projection onto one level of all of human
reality, but the encounter remains a multi-dimensional
event that concerns the entire vital space. Human inter-
course always aims at a totality, of sympathy or an-
tipathy, consent or refusal. Here, language goes beyond
language. The static nature of the established language
furnishes the pretext and occasion for the dynamics of
an unending struggle for influence because neither
separation itself, disagreement, nor death can interrupt

this dialogue of experiences once two persons have confronted one another and so long as one of the parties remains alive.

Language, then, by its very nature seems to escape determination. Or rather, a very special effort is necessary to determine language. This is an effort with which the technicians of the more positivistic disciplines are preoccupied, engaged as they are in defining a precise formula in which each term says exactly what it says, and nothing more. Mathematical symbolization, chemical notations and all the technical languages represent, then, more or less perfect attempts at a universal and objective exposition in which the meaning of each expression is defined in a narrowly restrictive sense. Over against this language that says all that can be said is the language that says nothing of what can be said, or almost nothing—the language of intimacy where innuendo predominates, where each word indicates an attitude and evokes a possibility of interior adventure. Between the contrasting limits of explicit and implicit language—between speaking exhaustively and silence —there is a hierarchy of the usual forms of hints and reticences. And one can argue endlessly whether the perfection of human speech is found in the language which says most or in the one which says least. Besides, perhaps the language that says the most is after all the one that says the least—a language based on the objectivity of things but not on the personality of human beings, an inhuman language.

Nevertheless, it is evident that language, bound to the presence of others, an opening to others, contributes at the same time to the constitution of personal being. All communication is bound up with a moment of awareness. The detour through others always leads me

back to myself. In the reciprocity of speaking and listen-
ing dormant possibilities are actualized within me: each
act of speaking, whether spoken or merely understood,
is the opportunity for an awakening, the discovery perhaps of a value the appeal of which I had not been
aware. Etymologically, the notion of *con*-sciousness
calls to mind an image of emergence from solitude, the
pairing of a being *with*. There is a creative power in
communication of which an isolated man feels pain-
fully deprived. Such was the testimony of Wagner, who,
during a painful period in his life, wrote to one of his
friends:

> "Deprived of all stimulation from the tangible world, con-
> tinually reduced to feeding on myself, I need, in order
> somewhat to maintain my vital energy, most active and
> encouraging relations with the external world: after all,
> whence then would come to me the desire to communi-
> cate the depths of my being if I should encounter silence
> everywhere around me?" [2]

Communication therefore has a creative power. It
gives self-awareness to each in the reciprocal relation
with the other. It is in the world of speech that the
edification of personal life is realized, communion between persons always being presented in the form of a
making explicit of value. The saving grace of communication, wherein one gives by receiving or receives by
giving, is the discovery of one's fellow man, of one's
neighbor—that other self, in friendship or love, more
real than myself because he is identified with the value
discovered through out meeting. Each gives the other
essential hospitality in his better self; each recognizes

2. Wagner, *Lettres à Hans de Bulow*, trans. Knoff, Cres, 1928,
p. 15.

the other and receives from him that same recognition without which human existence is impossible. For, reduced to himself, man is much less than himself; whereas, in the light of openness to the other, the possibility of an unlimited growth is offered to him.

VII / Expression

BEFORE I CAN BEGIN speaking, language must in one way or another be given to me by others. But if language is a hyphen, a calling-into—it is also a calling-forth, a calling-out. The relation to others is only meaningful insofar as it reveals that personal reality within the person who is himself speaking. To communicate, man *ex-presses* himself, i.e. he actualizes himself, he creates from his own substance, like the fruit one squeezes in order to get juice from it. The myth of the pelican feeding the young from its own breast gives us another and more sublime example of the same image to characterize poetic expression.

The expressive function of human speech balances its communicative function; it controls certain essential aspects of our experience. At the beginning of a life, expression seems to predominate. From the first cry of the infant to all those vocal activities before the acquisition of language, the preponderance of the first person over the second or the third is manifest. True, the cry is an appeal, but it remains within the personal reality it expresses. Even after the initial stages of education, childish language remains largely self-centered; babbling, playing with words, and verbal pastimes are situated outside of the realm of practical utility and social reality. It is only after the age of seven—"the age of reason" of traditional wisdom—that we can see in children's speech, psychologists tell us, the preponderance of the communicative over the simply expressive function. Expression, then, is considered to prevail at the beginning of life. Likewise, it prevails when speech achieves its greatest intensity: in passion or in terror, the *cry*, disengaged from all social inhibition, obeys an essential spontaneity of being. And, on a different plane, the *song* of the poet presents a more secret and purer speech, free from external contaminations, a sublimated cry wherein expression reaches its epitome.

Within these limits, expression is always present as a coefficient of speech, and is said to form a balance with that other coefficient, communication. For the need to express oneself to disappear, the very taste for life must be stricken. "I am no longer curious about what life can bring to me," André Gide remarks in one of his final pages. "I have more or less said well what I thought I had to say and I am afraid of repeating myself. . . ." [1] And this great writer, after noting that he has nothing more to say, immediately raises the question of suicide for himself. Thus each old man prepares himself for death by practicing the ultimate silence. A living man, writer or not, always has something to say, as a contribution to the reality of the world in which his task is to declare himself.

Just as a face devoid of all expression would no

1. *La Nouvelle Revue Francaise*, Hommage a André Gide, 1951, pp. 371–72.

longer be a human face, so too the whole person appears to us as an expressive being, in other words as the origin of intentions that are appropriate to him and that permit him to transform the environment. Moreover, speaking is only one of the means of expression, the most perfect perhaps, but still not the only one. An actor's education calls for apprenticeship in mime and gesture. Deprived of voice, and with even his face masked, the student must become capable of representing various human feelings simply by the use of his body. But even more, his behavior can evoke on the bare stage various landscapes: prairie, mountain, forest, sunlight, rain, mud. . . . Therefore, the magic of human presence, reduced to the play of bodily expression, suffices to suggest a landscape. Now the actor's exercise reproduces in the abstract an affirmation which each of us ceaselessly and unconsciously radiates around himself. We are world centers. Our behavior and moods give meaning, at any given moment, to the environment of beings and things. That which is called the personality of a man or of a woman is reflected in the decor of his life, a decor which is the sedimentation of his behavior, the inscription of an existence on the world.

Thus the function of expression consists in a movement of man outside himself in order to give meaning to the real. Expression is the act of man establishing himself in the world, in other words adding himself to the world. It is the duty of each to so create his own balance, or to recover it, bringing his inner resources into play when the balance is upset. Language, by erupting toward the stars, thereby allows us to come down to earth. It has the power to re-establish us if we are abruptly cut off from our usual securities. Such is the function of the least elaborated speech in which expression takes place in a pure state independently of all discursive intelligibility. All the different kinds of cry, howl, exclamation, interjection, and oath are attempts to adapt the self to a world that is slipping away. Surprise, joy, fear, and terror give rise to purely emotional speech. Expression is condensed at its most intense, a catastrophic reaction, a desperate attempt to face the disordering of circumstances that strikes us with a radical disorientation. Faced with anguish, torture, or death, when a man no longer has anything human to affirm, his cry remains the only testimony of which he is still capable, a testimony in which evocation and invocation are mixed together in an ultimate call of consciousness. Stripped of all other means, he now can only count on the magical efficacy of the clamoring of his cry to save the situation.

Even in this extreme case, expression still seems to be tied to the need to establish a correspondence between the interior and the exterior. Man cannot live in isolation. His being is not defined by enclosing himself, but by shining forth—that is to say by his capacity at each moment to impose a form on the environment. A person, even when he thinks that he is denying himself to the world, doesn't stop expressing himself. When he wants to conceal a secret, he behaves like a man with a secret, the refusal to communicate being expressed as the very meaning of his behavior. Nothing is completely true for us as long as we cannot announce it to the world as to ourselves. Advertising is part of our joy and our suffering: the lover cannot prevent himself from proclaiming his happiness, the convert his faith, or the unfortunate his despair. Expression doesn't intervene here as a secondary element; it is the source of awareness of his adventure for the hero. The ultimate sense of a secret is perhaps found in our nostalgia for freely revealing it. And the kingdom of God that all men dream of in their own way would undoubtedly be the universal revelation of each to everyone else.

Obviously, we are not there yet, but the whole of human experience in its militant sense may be understood as a striving for expression. Sainte-Beuve, a man of letters, said that for a certain kind of mind, "writing is deliverance." Such is the way of the writer: the discipline of expression frees him from the spectres which haunt him. A victim of his own unfortunate love, Werther dies, but Goethe is saved. And Hugo prevails over the suffering for his Leopoldine by dint of immortal verse. Not all men write, but all resort to the power of expression in speech or in action to overcome inner threats, to check the idle temptations of care or suffering. Speaking here indicates a stepping-back. The decision to express marks the threshold between the passivity of eating one's heart out and creative activity. To speak, to write, to express is to act, to survive crisis, to begin living again, even when one thinks it is only to relive one's sorrow. Expression is a kind of exorcism because it crystallizes the resolve not to let oneself go.

The example of the poet is particularly significant insofar as it carries to its maximum the striving for expression in language. The writer is a man who speaks in the sense that he must establish himself by the use he makes of speaking, the impersonality of the established tongue giving way to the power of suggestion of personal being. But the language of the poet in his mastery is not a regression to infantile egocentrism, where communication gives way completely to expression. In the case of the poet, it is necessary for expression to have the support of others, and for it to establish a new communication between an author and his readers. The writer, in order to be understood, must start with the language of everyone else; but, if he has genius, he will use this language as no one before him has used it. This reconquest of language corresponds to the creation of a *style* in which the personality of the poet is created at the same time that it is expressed.

The poet is the man who rediscovers speech thanks to a discipline that returns him to himself. The established language is a devalued language because the chief characteristic of community is to reduce value to the status of an object. It is a pruned language, having become a mere common denominator, a centrifugal language because its center is everywhere and its circumference nowhere. The poet brings about the restitution of the word. He restores resonance to speech, he offers each word in a new situation, and in such a way that its original power reappears. "To give a purer meaning to the words of the tribe," the plan of Mallarmé, is the plan of the genius, thanks to which the most commonly used words mysteriously rediscover their original integrity and become animated by a phospherescent glow. Living speech has freed them from their captivity at the heart of a dead tongue. The poet gives words their due even as he reduces them to the discipline of style.

In addition, the play of words infinitely transcends itself here. The benefit of this style is that the discipline does not remain simply formal. By working over words, one discovers ideas. To pay attention to each word, with an eye to avoiding the ambiguities and vagaries of everyday speech, is to pay attention to the real and to oneself. Concern for the right expression is bound up with concern for true reality: accuracy (*justesse*) and integrity (*justice*) are two related virtues. It is never a question of the universe of discourse alone because any construction, even architecture, is a construction of man. The truth of this fact is indicated in literature by the cease-less heroism necessary in pursuing the struggle for style. The effort never ceases; at the slightest relaxation, the new form degenerates into a formula. There comes a moment when the power is lost, when style seems an empty imitation of itself, a whole jumble of conditioned responses in which the person is the victim rather than the master. The great artist avoids imitating even him-self. He continually undertakes the task of remaining vigilantly aware of the world and words, a task forever unfinished because the world changes and is renewed, and living man with it.

The power of style, then, is not the privilege of the poet alone. The writer seems to us testimony to man in his enterprise to impose his mark on the environment. Style expresses the *thread of life,* the movement of a destiny according to its creative meaning. The cele-brated words of Buffon: "style is the very man" must be understood in the fullest sense. Style establishes man, not simply the style of speaking or writing, but the style of living in general. A person gives himself away in each of his attitudes: one looks after his words as one looks after his clothing. We can look after each of our mo-ments, or else abandon them to a slipshod attitude that indicates a lack of personal discipline, just as do bad manners and poor dress. The struggle for style may here stand as a definition of the whole personality since it is the undertaking of giving an appropriate value to each moment of self-affirmation. Man's presence to himself and the world in his own present raises a constant problem for him. For no solution will put an end to the search, and appropriateness (justesse) here is a matter of taste, constantly threatened with falling short or going too far: it isn't far from simplicity to studied elegance and affectation, from refinement to coyness or preciousness. The gift of proper expression is the privilege of certain beings who intuitively know the balance-point and show, in the face of the most unexpected difficulty, that they are equal to the circumstances.

Thus style is the peculiar expression of personality. If it be true that language is a world, it is also true that the world is a language that must conform to the influence of personal authenticity. To be original is to be an origin, a beginning, and to stamp the situation with one's mark. That doesn't mean that it is enough, like the young fashion-plate, Alcibiades, to have one's dog's tail cut off, or to lisp in the manner of the dandies in the Directoire period. The virtue of originality does not consist in attracting attention to oneself by any means whatsoever. Originality is not turned outward, but inward. It corresponds to the concern for proper expression, to honesty in self-expression. In this sense, it behooves each to give himself his language, to find his style. Each person's *Weltanschauung* is a view that belongs only to him; style signifies the task given to man of becoming aware of perspective. Each of us, even the most simple of mortals, is charged with finding the expression to fit his situation. Each of us is charged with realizing himself in a language, a personal echo of the language of all which represents his contribution to the human world. The struggle for style is the struggle for consciousness (*la vie spirituelle*).

VIII / The Authenticity of Communication

PERFECT EXPRESSION would signify for a person the full manifestation of what he is, with no reservation. Perfect communication would consist of a communion with others in which personality would lose the sense of its own limits. It is clear, as we have shown, that expression cannot be complete without the consciousness of being understood, and that community has value only if it puts into play the resources of each of those existences which it unites. One nostalgia offers to man two different but alternative faces of a single desire for absoluteness. From this point of view, the experience of speaking would be the experience of a failure. Instead of being at the service of the patent requirements of both expression and communication together, it seems that language creates insurmountable obstacles to their complete satisfaction.

This new reproach against language has nothing to do with integrity or lack of integrity (*la bonne ou mauvaise foi*). It is no longer a matter here of finding fault with established injustice and moral and social disorder, but becoming conscious of a constitutional limitation of human speech, an ontological lack. Words are very imperfect means of communication: very often they conceal instead of reveal, and they screen man when he dreams of perfect transparency. Every man feels unrecognized and misunderstood; and every man desires, in those hours of melancholy, another medium of understanding. It would be a medium in which speech would be song, and song would be spontaneously faithful to the most subtle inflections of the soul. The need to speak, so Plotinus considers, is the punishment for a fall that has deprived the creature of his original perfection. It will disappear once this perfection is rediscovered in a better world:

> "We certainly cannot think of them (souls free of the body), it seems to me, as employing words when, though they may occupy bodies in the heavenly region, they are essentially in the Intellectual: and very surely the deliberation of doubt and difficulty which they practice here must be unknown to them There; all their act must fall into place by sheer force of their nature; there can be no question of commanding or of taking counsel; they will know, each, what is to be communicated from another, by present consciousness. Even in our own case here, eyes often know what is not spoken; and There all is pure, every being is, as it were, an eye, nothing is concealed or sophisticated, there is no need of speech, everything is seen and known." [1]

For the mystic, language imposes a gulf between one soul and another, between the soul and God. The world of speech thus may be considered a universe of generalized relativity where salvation is only possible by the

1. Plotinus, *Enneades,* trans. Stephen Mackenna (London, 1956), IV, 3, 18.

grace of escaping it. The insufficiency of language, moreover, coincides with the insufficiency of the world itself. Nothing here on earth measures up to our aspirations; our real home is elsewhere. Such, revived through the ages, has been the complaint of a spiritualism incapable of enduring the slavery of corporeality. To speak one's thought, one's love, or one's faith has been thought of as a betrayal of them; there can be truth only within. Language makes us keep our noses to the ground, it opposes all elevation. "That a man has the right to speak about the weather," writes Kierkegaard, "I know, but another question has concerned me all my life. . . . There is a silent relationship by means of which we are bound to God and which is shattered if we converse with another about that which is of such importance to us." [2]

That objection to language in its very essence casts everything in doubt once again. In fact, in most cases, it still seems that language realizes what one expects of it, i.e. understanding between the speakers. But the nature of that understanding must be reconsidered. Everyday speech embodies an exchange of news, advice, messages and the like. Except for misunderstanding, which can always be corrected, we succeed pretty well in coming to agreement when it is a matter of sharing the daily task of living and working together. The success of this pragmatic language is extended and expanded in the case of scientific language: physicists, chemists, and mathematicians can converse amongst themselves in perfect understanding. Their problems are resolved by the simple elucidation of the technical formulas they have at their command, formulas moreover that they are free to enrich if need be.

The success of this language is due to the fact that

2. Kierkegaard, *Journal*, 1850.

each term corresponds to a given meaning and that this determination itself is established in a horizon common to the individuals in communication. Two engineers confront each other within the closed field of a precisely defined vocabulary, so that any dispute that may arise between them is subordinate to a previous agreement that extends far beyond it. The same is true in the daily life of a family or a working group. Here, the exchange of words takes place against the background of a general understanding—less rigorously formalized than that which supports Euclidian geometry or the technique of building with poured concrete—but nonetheless sufficiently defined by a mutual and tacit consent. Family life as well as the professional life find in language a docile instrument as long as they stay at the level of average meanings codified by usage. Weekend travelers, thrown together by chance in the compartment of an excursion train, can chat with no trouble at all. They understand one another perfectly.

But, someone will object, if these people understand one another so well, it is because they have nothing to say. They have been attuned to one another in advance by their common insignificance. The *commonplaces* which they spout with easy assurance take the place of personality for them. As for scientists and technicians, they too have in a different way given up their personal affirmation in order to be converted to the unity of an objective system. There is no risk of misunderstanding between them for the good reason that, as long as they play the game, they all say the same thing. Men can agree only by avoiding difficulty, in other words by refusing to be themselves in order to play the role of soloists in the same collective choir. All language has by constitution the quality of common denominator. To speak then is to alienate oneself in order to mingle with everyone else. There is no language for originality—that is to say for difference, for personality.

This is the point of view developed with such penetration and force by such thinkers as Kierkegaard and, more recently, Karl Jaspers. Their thesis amounts to showing that the activity of speaking brings about the substitution for each of the speakers in dialogue a kind of average, impersonal individual. Putting it another way, language can only express the exteriority of beings and things. It categorically refuses to express inwardness. For all speaking is *publication,* publicity. It indicates recourse to an intermediary, to a *means* of expression in the place of immediate contact, from soul to soul. When two beings are present to one another, language gets in the way and falsifies their harmony. The desire for personal authenticity requires the application to language of the principle, two is company and three is a crowd. For common words and accepted ideas constantly impose their undesirable presence and the surveillance of those absent ones who are always wrong.

Thus, on this point there may be said to be a congenital insufficiency of human speech. Of my thought, I can only show the exterior, the surface. The core slips away because the core is not an idea or thing, but the attitude that is peculiar to me, the intention of my whole life. This horizon of my being cannot be made explicit, and yet it is with respect to it that the meaning of everything I can say is established. Thus I cannot publicize my better self, and insofar as two existences cannot absolutely coincide, I do not have any means to gain access to the best of others. Thus each man remains for all others a secret. There cannot be any direct agreement, any full understanding. The schoolmaster gives instruction to his students, but his published and objective doctrine is not the best of his influence. Outside of and in spite of discourse, a contact is established between teacher and student. It is a dialogue without words, and different in each situation, a hidden dialogue, the only decisive one. There is thus a mystery to the influence of great teachers. A Socrates and more recently an Alain exercised on their students a veritable fascination, different in each case, and each time exclusive. It was an influence of which the readers of the writings of Alain or the contemporary accounts of Socrates scarcely have any idea. Along the same lines, the presence of Jesus signified for each of his followers a direct and living relation at the heart of which speaking became a call, an encounter of being with being, and the few words actually said only give a vague approximation of it.

The efficacy of speaking may be said therefore to stumble upon an insuperable limit. Words do not give direct access to personal truth. At best, they can but point the way. The explicit teaching of the master counts for less than his example, the spell of a gesture or a smile. The rest is silence, because the last word, the key word of a man, is not a word. The truest communication between men is *an indirect communication,* that is to say it operates in spite of language, by means of chance—and often in exactly the opposite sense. The ultimate refuge in each of us is the domain to which words have no access. The soul is there alone in shadow and silence, with that "strange certainty," evoked by the poet, Rilke, "that anything more than a beautiful mediocrity, essentially incapable of progress, will after all have to be accepted, experienced and overcome in the

most complete solitude, as by someone infinitely isolated, almost unique." [3]

The theme of indirect communication is bound up
with a conception of man that insists on the secret core
of each life. Silence is truer than speech. The poets and
often writers have insisted on a wall of inexpressibility
which their greatest efforts of expression run up against.
The very obscurity of the great poets, the obscure lives of
a Rimbaud, a Mallarmé, and a Valéry confirm the para-
dox of a disclosure necessary and yet impossible. Baudelaire, borrowing an image from Poe, expresses under the
title, "my heart stripped bare," this desire for an epiph-
any, for a total self-revelation which would also be the
long-sought salvation. But the darkness is not dissi-
pated. The more one speaks the more one says nothing.
The more one strives to say something, the more one is
buried in an irremediable silence. If the body be a tomb
and if the world be a dungeon, language is as well a
prison that walls us up in ourselves, all the more cruelly
because it seemed that it ought to free us entirely.

The whole corpus of shared philosophic, artistic, and
mystical insights points to a real but no longer insuperable difficulty. A more precise analysis of the conditions
of dialogue ought to permit us, in effect, to go beyond
this moment of despair. The most pressing need is to
grasp speech in the context of the particular situation in
which it emerges. A sentence is not uttered in a vacuum: it presupposes a certain state of relations between
the speakers, and the horizon of a language corresponding to shared values. In ordinary usage, the context is taken for granted, so that the literal text seems to
be self-sufficient. Familiar conversation or the newspa-

3. Rilke, *Letter of Nov. 4, 1909,* from the French translation
by Pitrou.

per article are based on an existing language, determined once and for all as a function of tacitly accepted average values. Talking at cross-purposes and misunderstanding only show up when one of the persons present repudiates that implicit mutual consent and denounces the social pact of everyday language. An automatic and approximative speech gives way, then, to authentic speech, which runs into all sorts of obstacles.

The examination of this authentic speech will nevertheless allow us to isolate the implications of valid language. The meaning of speaking depends, indeed, upon three distinct elements, the totality of which alone justifies it. First of all, one must consider *who* is speaking. In this respect, by virtue of what is the speaker speaking? Is he a man who lives hand-to-mouth, the man of the passing moment, scattering his words like seeds to the wind? Or rather is he committed to what he says, and to what degree? There is thus a personal characteristic that measures the intensity of speech. It can reveal being: promises and oaths directly affirm an inner value attitude in which a man comes to be one with what he says. But most of our sentences do not present that intimate tension; they are more or less disengaged from personal being. A proper appreciation must try to estimate the amount of authenticity which speaking man confers on his speech.

But the reference alone to him who speaks remains one-sided: one must also take into account the other, him *to whom* the phrase is directed. That object is essential, because the spoken word is truly efficacious only if there is a reciprocity between the speakers. If they do not find themselves in agreement, but out of step with each other, misunderstanding will necessarily arise. The literal meaning of the words perhaps will be understood, but their value-meaning will escape. If someone thinks I am serious when I joke, or humorous when I am most sincere, my words lose their meaning on route. A deep and intense declaration, a confession or a cry from the heart are as difficult to listen to as they are to say. For real communication to be achieved, there must be the same enthusiasm on both sides, a kind of preliminary communion. Each time that I speak, what I say depends upon the other whom my language intends: an indifferent person, an adversary, or a friend and ally. Meaning is always the trait of a collaboration.

Thirdly, that collaboration itself doesn't take place in a vacuum. The *moment* is the third dimension of any verbal expression. Each act of speaking is in its own way situational, each word is an historic word. The situation suffices to give value to any remark, which then becomes decisive because it is pronounced in a decisive moment. For example, some dying words might never have been remembered by humanity if they had not been the last words of some historically illustrious person.

Thus a sound exegesis must not be content to consider a man's every word, to somehow reduce his words to a single plane. One must carry out a kind of study in relief. It must be a study in which the statement each time takes on form and life according to the degree of personal commitment of the man who is speaking, according to the reciprocity of the encounter and according to the meaning of the moment. The apparent meaning of the speech gives way to its personal value. Besides, such an evaluation can only be carried out by those in whom the very sense of the situation is in some way restored. The extreme speech of a crisis only takes on its full meaning in a complimentary critical situation. All true understanding is itself an accomplishment. The hero speaks to heroes, the poet to poets, and the appeal of the saint is only effective if it releases in us a dormant possibility of saintliness. Non-comprehension is a bar opposed to the demands of others, and at the same time a specification of one of our limits. So too we can become strangers to ourselves. Because one's life, at any given moment carried to the heights of awareness of value, can fall back into its customary mediocrity, we can cease to understand this or that attitude which once was ours, this or that promise we have made. Then it is that we renounce *keeping our word*. Like the voice that breaks because it is incapable of holding to a high note, we find ourselves incapable of holding to the locus of values that, at one time, enlightened us. Criticism of language, then, must not consider that it is flat, and must not start with the idea that anyone at all can say anything at all, to anyone else, at any old time. Thinkers who insist on the indirect character of communication ordinarily make a kind of fetish of proper language, as if truth were an intrinsic character of speaking. Now speech is not true in itself. Speaking is only an in-between, a linking between man and man through time. Language is defined as a means of communication. It is not communication itself. The condemnation of speaking is ordinarily founded upon the intellectualist prejudice that truth must be expressed in discourse, whereupon it is shown without too much trouble that no discourse is in fact the equivalent of truth. Imagine if you will certain impassioned cross-examinations or trials in which the alleged culprit is admonished, for example, *to tell the truth*. Now, in spite of the apparently sincere efforts of the questioners and the questioned, the impression remains that what is essential has not been disclosed. Substantially, everything has been said. But a mystery remains, a human mystery that language doesn't manage to clear up. The facts are established, but the intentions of the main characters remain vague because they themselves are not clear. The journalist who witnesses the trial indicates in conclusion that "the truth will never be known." The fault is not in the language: if the truth can be expressed here at all, it is that it is not a saying, but a being and a doing.

Communication is thus only indirect if one claims initially to identify language and being, as if it were sufficient merely to say words to have being change with them. Now, value is not in the language, but in the man who tries by every means to make the best of himself. Speech can contribute to this self-education of man, to this revelation of his being, but only in a secondary sense. Words are not magical and do not do away with the need for personal effort. They are a landmark along that difficult road which is the progressive realization of man according to truth. The idea of an absolutely perfect language is as false as the idea of an absolutely just man. Living man is a man on the way, a way that consists of continually re-establishing a balance that keeps destroying itself. Speech is a particularly valuable symbol of this perpetual movement of human being, a movement that is opposed to any definitive formulation.

Thus is justified the experience of the *inexpressible*, which the desire of the writer for expression often runs up against. Total expression would be the actualization of all possibilities, the liberation of all the competitors for being that make up a personal reality—a kind of unravelling of man. Such an experience would presuppose a going to the limit, an idea of which may be given by certain particularly tense moments of existence: the panoramic vision of the dying, for example, which is supposed to apprehend in an instant the whole of a lifetime. That situation transcends the plane of speaking as well as the normal order of human life.

Words offer us props for the realization of what we are. But our last words are not merely a string of words. The final words that seal a communion or the final consent to love and to truth assume a long experience of self-relation and relation to others. They are the reward for a striving to live that they can't absolve one from. The man worthy of the name doesn't accuse language of being constitutionally insufficient. He struggles with himself in order to have access to language, in order to give speech to the best of his being. The great poet is not the one who proclaims, "The most beautiful lines are those that will never be written. . . ." The most beautiful lines are those that have been written by those poets most able to struggle with language and reduce it to obedience. The great writer, a Balzac or a Dostoevsky for example, triumphs over the inexpressible not when he denounces it, but when he expresses it. The would-be genius, incapable of actualizing it, is only a dreamer who looks for alibis for his ineffectiveness. The passage from the possible to the real provides the effective measure of every man beyond the inconsistency of dreams. In this sense, there is no difference between language and thought, because language *is* thought: a thought poorly expressed is an inadequate thought.

It is in the same way that obscurity, for which writers are often reproached, should be understood. The naive reader rebels because he cannot understand this or that literary text as easily as a newspaper article. He will quite freely accuse the author of having intentionally obscured his writings. But authentic obscurantism, in painting, in music, and in literature as well, is only the counterpart of the struggle by the artist to affirm an original vision of the world. The discipline of a style corresponds to a need for precision that removes the creator from all the ready-made formulas of the established language. He has had to pass from the common meaning to the particular meaning that is his, sometimes at the cost of an heroic struggle. In order to understand the works of a Monet, a Debussy, a Mallarmé, or a Claudel, the amateur must give of himself. The effort of the creator demands in reciprocity an analogous effort: communication involves a sharing of the difficulty. Now the average reader or the everyday listener or spectator believes that he can obtain effortlessly what has caused the creator so much trouble to bring into being. He will always prefer the fashionable writer or artist who speaks and feels like everyone else. The obscurity of the new language, however, will progressively diminish as its creative originality has engendered a new everyday meaning. The innovators of yesterday are the classics of today, now that their new and difficult language has been established and has become the language of everyone.

The idea of indirect communication, then, would seem to be in need of reinterpretation insofar as it seems to indict language when it is the very nature of man that is in question. In short, it is not communication that is indirect—it is man himself. The limits of expression and communication are the very limits of personal being. The ever-recurrent themes of *silence* and *secrecy* must themselves be understood from this point of view. Undoubtedly, there does exist a human secrecy. This is because first of all one cannot say everything without annihilating oneself, and secondly because on the plane of speech as well as in all other areas determination is negation. But this secret is only the vague borderline between the real and the virtual, between fact and value, between the present and the future. It is not a bar opposed to expression, but a point of departure and the very stuff of personal affirmation. Likewise, the apology for silence, which holds it to be more eloquent, richer, and more definitive than any words can be, is founded on a confusion. Silence is not in itself a particularly dense form of expression. It has meaning only at the core of an existing communication as a counterpart to it, or as the final sanction of an established language. There are silences of poverty and absence as well as pregnant silences—and it is not the silence that makes this latter full. Human relations must have progressed by other means to that point of perfection at which words become useless for fostering the communication. Thus, silence possesses no intrinsic magic: it is a blank in the dialogue where the harmonics of the existing accord or discord may appear. Silence gives voice to the depths, when they are in play, and to distances, if there are any.

In place of the notion of indirect communication, then, we must substitute that of a greater or lesser authenticity of communication. In other words, there is no fixed frontier of language, but there are frontiers of man, frontiers that it behooves every person to extend as far as he thinks fit. Language is one of the agents of our incarnation. Within it are embodied the needs of man struggling to express themselves. *The* human labor is the endeavor to be present to the world and the pursuit of values. According to a fine expression of the German philosopher, Jaspers, the will to communicate is the faith of the philosopher. It is a desire to communicate and to communicate oneself, in spite of all obstacles. It is a will to achieve a state of peace among men, that is to say, beyond misunderstandings and violence, that full understanding which extends into and is verified by effective cooperation.

IX / The World of Speaking

FOR MAN, speaking is the beginning of existence, a self-affirmation in the social and moral orders. Before speech, there is only the silence of organic life, a silence that is nevertheless not a silence of death, for all of life is communication, and even before birth the embryo is part of the maternal biological cycle. But the embryo or the newborn, walled up within its organic impressions, can only know a dependent existence. The affirmation of individuality begins when it has stepped back, when speech confers on it the double capacity of *evocation* of self and *invocation* of others. Human being is a being in participation, and the experience of solitude is only a certain way of being aware of the absence of others within one's very presence. Personal reality is not constituted as a fundamental identity opposed to the multitude. Rather, it proceeds from plurality lived on the level of communication toward the progressive constitution of a self-consciousness as the center of relations.

To speak is to wake up, to move toward the world and others. Speaking actualizes an emergence thanks to

[93]

which man escapes the captivity of the environment. "Open, Sesame." Every word is a magical word opening an entrance or exit door from the past to the future. Speech inaugurates a new kind of reality. It is developed in a field of forces governed by a new physics with laws of conservation peculiar to it.

Nothing is more significant in this respect than the situation of man deprived of vocal communication with others. The person who is congenitally deaf is also mute because the ear is the teacher of the voice. That deficiency of means of communication well illustrates the fact that speaking is not merely a means to an end. The lack of vocal communication leads to an almost total paralysis of intelligence. Deaf-mutes used to be reduced to a kind of idiocy, a vegetable existence, at least until the day when someone discovered the means of re-establishing in indirect ways the communication they lack. By being given speech, they were made human beings. No less convincing is the evidence of those stricken by deafness after a long and normal life. The torments of a Beethoven or a Marie Lenéru show that their affliction is more terrible even than blindness—as Montaigne had anticipated: "If I were now forced to choose," he said, "I would rather consent, I believe, to losing my sight than my hearing or speech." [1] Indeed, sight puts us in touch with nature, but hearing is the sense peculiar to the human world. To convince oneself of this, it is sufficient to plug one's ears on a day when one is in the midst of an animated group of people. This experience of artificial deafness renders the behavior of those present completely unintelligible. It would seem then that gestures, attitudes, and all kinds of mimicry are only corrolaries of the voice. Speaking is the prin-

1. Montaigne, *Essays*, III, 8.

ciple dimension of expression. To take speech away is to make of human reality a kind of silent and absurd film. The affliction of the deaf person brings about a kind of exile whereas the blind man remains attached to the community. Indeed, the blind person arouses the compassion of everyone while the deaf person is ridiculous. Those "funny deaf stories" indicate an alienation through a social viciousness which is never exercised against the blind man. There are no funny stories about blind men. . . .

Speaking is therefore the human function of social integration. A sociology of speech is a must if one wants to explore the human reality of language, considered here as the proper dimension of communication. The field of study thus opened seems extremely vast insofar as it includes extremely varied structures and intentions. First of all, that language which joins several persons together in more or less complete understanding presupposes a common frame of reference, a frame that is given initially and that is constantly revised by the development of communication. But this frame of reference itself is not simple, and its complexity seemingly increases with analysis. Its first and most obvious form is that of *vocabulary* and *grammar:* the exchange of words implies the tacit recognition of a language guaranteed by a social authority. And the use of the tongue implies certain rules of thought. People cannot understand each other in argument or even in simple conversation if there is no agreement on the rules for the articulation of thoughts, on the appropriateness or inappropriateness of ideas in relation to one another. The common usage of speech presupposes that other social pact of a *logic,* the whole body of norms for the discipline of reason.

But this ideal of a simply formal truth does not guarantee relations between men. Another sense of validity arises to authorize our agreements or our disagreements. A higher jurisdiction becomes evident beyond opinions, a jurisdiction that in the last resort is alone fit to bring order to thoughts. St. Augustine wrote:

> "When both of us see that what you say is true, when we both see that what I say is true—where do we see it, I ask you? Certainly, it is not in you that I see it, it is not in me that you see it. Both of us see it in immutable Truth, which is beyond our minds." [2]

The form names a content. The circulation of ideas in the exchange of words itself presupposes the mediation of metalogical values. A person affirms his fundamental attitudes in his obedience to the principles which make him what he is. Thus agreement at the level of vocabulary presupposes the recognition of certain rules of the game of thought, rules that are themselves subordinate to transcendent values at the level of which communion becomes possible.

Thus we see emerge a hierarchy of examples of communication by language. There are exchanges by fits and starts. It is a kind of communication that seems to be developed at the level of verbal automatism and mere vocabulary. Technical discussion in which one uses formal arguments may be considered more of the order of logic, whereas intimate conversations in which two personal lives confront one another without reservation takes place at the level of the values that control our varying destinies. However, we must not try here to establish rigidly clear-cut distinctions. Every use of speech to some degree implies all three of the phenom-

2. Augustine, *Confessions*, XII, 35.

ena we have isolated. For agreement about vocabulary cannot be achieved without the acceptance of certain formal structures, and the most rigorous logic only takes on meaning with reference to values. For example, there is nothing more passionate than the disputes of logicians, and the very precision of their intellectual methods scarcely seems to help them reach common solutions.

Thus it is important for a sound understanding of speech to distinguish the various usages of speech, as a function of which speech itself is developed. By so doing, various realms in the utilization of discourse become apparent. One can *begin to speak* because one is in agreement, as it were, to affirm and develop an already existing understanding with oneself and between oneself and others. Personal monologue or conversation is the quiet and allusive speech of intimacy, a speech in which logic scarcely arises since the community of values keeps nourishing the exchange of words. This is a peaceful and balanced speech, the recitative, alone or in dialogue, of a deep understanding. But one can also begin speaking in order to strive to achieve agreement with oneself or with others by means of a bonafide confrontation that illuminates possible misunderstandings. Here, expression is preponderate because it is necessary to make explicit the frame of reference by defining the terms of the vocabulary and by specifying the rules for the interrelation of ideas. Preoccupation with logic, then, appears in the foreground, although in the final analysis agreement or disagreement is the consequence of structures of value that form the fundamental attitudes of each. One can also speak in order to sway the other, in order to impose on him one's own point of view. Here collaboration yields to a kind of imperialism.

The role of technique in speaking reaches its high point. Rhetoric, dialectic, and sophistry, for example, represent traditional forms of an art of persuasion that makes logic the instrument of the desire for domination. To convince is to conquer.

The use of speech thus appears as a constitutive element of the encounter. Monologue, dialogue, conversation, polemic, sermon, or plea represent so many forms of coexistence between men. Once again let us make clear that words witness to being: for what is being played out in the world of speech is the very destiny of human souls.

X / Homo Loquens

IF ONE WANTS to enumerate the various
kinds of language, the simplest method without doubt is
to adopt a quantitative point of view. In every case, the
number of participants changes the laws and the very
nature of language, according to whether it is a monologue, a dialogue, a conversation with a greater or fewer
number of participants, or finally a mass phenomenon.
The *monologue* appears as the most limited form of this
sociology of speech. It is the language of a solitary
individual, an entirely personal use of language, and a
kind of introduction into the oratorical adventure. Psychologists and philosophers, at the end of the last century, were particularly interested in this initial form of
language, which they called "inward speech," and they
tried to define its relations to thought. Then novelists
took up the theme, reviving it in the form of works that
strove to reproduce the very flow of speaking consciousness. It was undoubtedly the Irishman James
Joyce who, after the Frenchman Dujardin and before the
American William Faulkner, most nearly perfected this

genre in his *Ulysses*. This enormous novel attempts to express the interior monologue of a single character during a typical day. The stream of consciousness within it takes on an epic flow that reminds one in its spontaneity of thought coming into being through the struggle for words.

Quite apart from any consideration of literature or esthetics, the very idea of interior monologue raises a human problem. Nothing is less certain than this identification of personal consciousness with an endless babbling, the ingenuousness of which, moreover, the writer considers the epitome of art. In any case, monologue is not the beginning of speech. Indeed, it might be considered a falling off from the normal level of speaking, an indication of an introversion or a withdrawal. It is a semi-subterranean speech, a solitary vice, for what one speaks to oneself one would not dare to *maintain* before others. The ins and outs of this form of thought obey the most primitive commands of our biological being: instincts and desires reign sovereign here. It is not the expression of the person, but of his cenesthesia, and at best it is the daydream of an existence that lacks the mature power to actualize itself.

At the same time, it is easy to show that the authentic intimacy of a self in relation to itself does not destroy the relation to others. Robinson Crusoe during his years of solitude, or more contemporaneously, Admiral Byrd buried alone for months in a polar observation post, are not cut off from the human community. Their monologue is not interior; rather, it is only an apparent monologue. Active and constructive thought doesn't cease referring to the real presence of others. This invocation of others will reach the person who is addressed with a certain delay, but it still intervenes as an intention and continues to animate the movement of thought. For each man, the naive attitude faced with a new and puzzling event occurs in the form: "I'll have to speak to so and so. . . ." And the moralist who made of conscience the "voice of God" meant that each of our moments presupposes an authoritative listener over against our solitary ruminations.

The point of departure for the use of speech, then, is not monologue, but *dialogue*. Man shouldn't be alone when speaking. Monologue is the beginning of madness, the confrontation of others the beginning of wisdom. As the Spanish critic, Eugenio d'Ors, wrote:

> "All monologue is by nature unkempt. Thanks to dialogue, the soul of others penetrates into our own, as a comb digs its teeth into the tangles of disordered hair. It penetrates it, straightens it out, and tidies it up." [1]

The image is ingenious. It calls to mind the effectiveness of *dia*logue to render meditation *intel*-ligible, that is to say to permit the solitary individual to read between the lines of his own naturally confused thought. Indolent fantasy gives way to obedience, for the other exercises a veritable shaping of my consciousness that, beyond the exchange of words, establishes a real collaboration. The other voice is not limited to the role of accompaniment or mere echo. It becomes the educator of the first voice in this learning of coexistence.

Dialogue, therefore, is the first and most crucial test of universality. If I desire to reach understanding with others and to have them share my certainty, I must proceed to portion out the difficulty step by step so as to keep both minds in unbroken contact. When the listener

1. Eugenio d'Ors, *Au Grand Saint Christophe,* from the French translation by Mallerais, Corrêa, p. 117.

doesn't follow a train of thought, one must go back and lead him along, over ond over again, until he understands. Thus Socrates, that midwife to minds, proceeds from question to answer, following the roundabout ways of the ironic method. But that illustrious example himself teaches us that the power of dialogue has limits. Socrates speaks. The listener, each time more edified, only intervenes from time to time to punctuate with respectful approval the dazzling developments of the master. This second voice only takes the part of pauses when the virtuoso must catch his breath. If authentic dialogue means to work together on an equal footing, Socrates, who takes over the dialogue, seems more like a person in monologue. If it were not for that, he would not be the father of philosophy, for one characteristic of the great philosopher is precisely his inability to reach agreement with others. In reality philosophical dialogues only come to an end when they are literary works, like the Platonic dialogues—fictional dialogues drawn up by a single author. In the same way, Malebranche, Berkeley, and Leibniz simply alternate the voices of their own thought. But when the philosopher encounters another philosopher who asks him to justify himself, the result is almost inevitably a dialogue between deaf men. Witness Descartes, for instance, in the face of the critics of the *Meditations,* Malebranche at grips with Mairan, or even a Kant or an Aristotle so completely lacking in understanding in the face of thought other than their own. The continual experience of philosophic societies would be proof enough, if it were called for, of the fact that the thinker is almost always a man who speaks alone and doesn't listen to what is said to him.

However, there is no reason here to be surprised or upset. In fact, philosophic dialogue brings into confrontation matured personalities for whom the game is already up. They limit themselves to expressing a consolidated thought which they can't deny without denying themselves. Now, conversions are rare. True dialogue presupposes an open and receptive attitude, as opposed to sterile discussions in which each participant limits himself to restating his convictions, without ever giving an inch, and in which, as a last resort, he ends up by playing hide-and-seek or by hurling insults in a desperate effort to have the last word. The value of dialogue is thus not inherent in the genre itself, as rationalists sometimes seem to think. A new dimension is opened up to the life of the mind—but in this instance it is like a loveless marriage that has lost most of its meaning. The conjugal dialogue can be reduced to a long chain of domestic scenes. It may wrap itself around the couple absorbed in each other in an exclusivism that divorces them from the rest of the world and becomes a kind of monologue of two, a monologue in which the individual egos add themselves together instead of interacting. Dialogue offers the possibility of salvation. But the passage here from the possible to the real presupposes a receptive attitude, an openness to the world and the other. The interchange of words doesn't mean very much if it is not founded on the recognition of other people. The distinctive sign of man in dialogue is that he listens as well as he speaks, if not better. That is the effect an attentive presence, a spiritual hospitality, as it were, that excludes the desire to dazzle or to conquer as well as the claim to sovereignty. Authentic dialogue characterizes the encounter of men of good will, each of whom testifies for the other, not to himself alone, but to their common values. That is why in the recent period of bondage [*i.e.* the occupation] the gift of dialogue already bore within itself an anticipated liberation. But these moments are rare, and are given only to those who are worthy of them. Most men exchange words without ever entering into dialogue. Commonplaces are the substance of their ideas, and the opinions prevalent in their little social circle take the place of values.

When the number of speakers goes beyond two, dialogue gives way to *conversation.* Intimacy decreases in proportion to the number of participants. The implicit frame of reference of conversation, the common denominator of the group, will be the less the more different individuals are brought into play. The more there are, the less is confided. And yet, conversation is one of the most significant modes of social being. Novelists have abundantly described it, but sociologists and psychologists seem not to have given it all the attention it merits. Its importance to French culture, indeed, cannot be exaggerated. "Society," over the years, has been based upon an ethic and liturgy of conversation that has profoundly influenced our literature and with which the very genius of the French tongue remains impregnated, as it were. To a foreigner, one of the distinctive signs of the Frenchman is the ease of his speech and the agility of his wit, both of which tend to make him stand out as a brilliant conversationalist.

It is not a question here, of course, of technical discussion bearing on a precise object and meant to arrive at a decision. Rather, we are dealing here with conversation as an orchestration of good wills coming together according to certain social norms. In short, it is a tapestry or mosaic, a kind of living needlework. Indeed, it is women who have always given life to the activity of conversation. In the middle ages, polite conversation was already known in milady's apartments, and the love-courts echoed, in elegiac style, the crude pastimes of the lords—the hunt, war, and tournaments. At the beginning of the Renaissance, little by little one sees the substitution of the *salon* for the closed field of the tournaments. Conversation becomes another and more distinguished sport, a tournament of wit gathered around a lady of quality: Marguerite of Navarre, the marchioness of Rambouillet, their numerous followers of the eighteenth century, not to mention the Madame Sebatiers and the Verdurins of the nineteenth. The reception room of the *"precieuses,"* the wit-factories, and the salon become the theaters for ritual celebrations where speech displays the verbal decor of a unique style of existence.

A new type of man is now created, the "gentleman" (*honnête homme*), fashioned and codified by the moralists of the seventeenth century, and precursor of the modern "man of the world." It is certainly not asked of every man that he be a brilliant speaker, but it is important that he cut a figure in the game. Sophistication becomes the very model for moral obligation. The gentleman, defined in the celebrated book by the Jesuit Baltasar Gracian, is the courtier. In vain will Pascal, who doesn't like people, rail against him and turn his virtues into vices. The very idea of politeness calls to mind community (*polis*). The refined man takes a vow to be good company, thereby opposing himself to nature and breaking away from the struggle for life. He does this in order worthily to uphold his role in this gracious dance, this ballet of wit in which each in his turn must know how to efface himself and make way for the affirmation of others. It is a discipline of mutual valuation in which each contributes so that the common work of all might be more polished. The French spirit and the classical French language, rich in its universal appeal, are the result of this gradual education and it is to it that we owe Mme. de Sévigné and Racine, La Bruyère and Montesquieu, and those conversationalists who dazzled Europe, a Voltaire, a Diderot, a Mallarmé, and a Valéry.

This chamber music of conversation, however, has its detractors, its consciencious objectors. They reproach it for being an artificial and false genre, for being merely witty fireworks which stifle the voice of the soul. Within it, *Animus* becomes the jailer of *Anima*. Whence, over the years, the protest of men of dialogue, of scholars, and of writers. A Rousseau, a Maurice de Guérin, a Vigny, a Tolstoi, and an André Gide are concerned about its profound influence, and they are undoubtedly also poor conversationalists. Conversation weighs heavily on them by obliging them to constantly put themselves outside themselves, by placing them in competition with others in a struggle to achieve a social alienation in which one triumphs only by losing oneself. The element of inauthenticity in conversation undoubtedly stems from the fact that it offers the speaker an audience, however limited. Within dialogue, the confronting personalities engage each other without that stepping back which would transform the interaction into a spectacle. It is the third person who constitutes the audience. Because of him and for him, dissimulation will arise and it will continue to increase as the number of listeners increases. The social usage of speech, for example that of the professor or the preacher, the lawyer or the politician, defines a new genre—*eloquence*. Here all reciprocity disappears. Only one person speaks, and because of his privileged position he has a formidable power to cast a spell over the mass of men, a power fortified by the formulas of an age-old rhetorical technique. The orator is in fact one of the characteristic types of western man. He represents in a certain sense the very ideal which classical culture tried to realize in molding its students. Until the beginning of the 20th century, secondary education culminated in the course of "rhetoric." Collegiate dissertations, in French as in Latin, bore the name "discourse" (*"discours"*), and professors of prose literature held chairs in "eloquence."

Our age has seen the oratorical character of education disappear. But it has as well seen the emergence of dictators whose speech cast over immense masses of men a magical spell, the likes of which had never before been seen. Our age distrusts demagogues. Jules Renard long ago wrote in his journal: "It is a great deal easier to speak to a crowd than to an individual." The orator drowns us in the mass. Man in the crowd is a fallen man, bendable in any direction. We fear the emotional exaltation of the totalitarian masses. More generally, the orator always seems to be trying to deceive. In fact, the orator is not someone who is talking before an audience of dummies. Rather, he claims to be the spokesman for those whom he addresses. The professor wants to be the voice of the whole class just as the lawyer that of the jury. What appears to be a monologue is really a kind of dialogue, but an unequal one. It is a struggle of influences, a struggle for influence in which self-deception (*la mauvaise foi*) quite often triumphs over integrity (*la bonne foi*). There may be orators who are honest, but the art of oratory is not. Speaking man, *homo loquens, homo loquax,* seems to be the showman of his own conscience, if not that of others, and by that means always suspect of inauthenticity. Even when one admires the artist, one is never very sure of the man, of that man always seeking approval, as if incapable of existing by himself. He is, after all is said and done, enslaved by the very public he controls.

It was the invention of printing that brought about the decline of the art of oratory. It revealed the fact that eloquence was captive to immediacy, enclosed in a present where values are confused. They are confused because they can't be measured over space and time, and they can't be set in an order that escapes emotional involvement. Cleverly manipulated instincts can always win out over reason. Truth is born of reflection, of that slow and fruitful return to self that magic illusions of eloquence all seek to prevent at any cost. The objection to the orator, then, would seem to lie in the fact that he is constantly in danger of putting the reality of the event ahead of the reality of the person.

XI / Techniques of Stabilizing Speech

"FOR THE GREEKS," wrote Fénelon, "everything depends on the people, and the people depend on speech." [1] The entirety of ancient culture is a culture of speech and it is within it that all authority is vested, and through it alone that power can be attained. The history of antiquity, and early man in general, only becomes intelligible to us if we take this all-important fact into account. In other words, there is an evolution of speech over time. The advent of new techniques expands its range, opening to it unknown dimensions which transform the very structure of existence. Man ceased to be simply a speaking being and became a writing and reading being. Thereby, the face of the world was transformed.

The emergence of humanity at all presupposed that first revolution which the passage from the lived to the spoken world constitutes. Human reality is defined first of all as a collection of designata, its unity is that of a vocabulary. The initial development of culture is speech

1. Fénelon, *Lettre à l'Académie*, IV.

[109]

in the process of expanding. This characteristic is enough to give us the key to the mythical consciousness, since the very word myth means speaking (*mythos*). Within this kind of life, speech is tied to a sustainer, i.e. the speech is of someone or other, it is spoken by someone. The only repository of speech, the only way to preserve it is personal memory; and like social memory, i.e. tradition and custom, personal memory is highly developed within the mythical culture. It is a culture of hearsay, of rumor, in which speech is all-powerful—a culture of formulas, secrets, and magic. Authority is the privilege of the wisemen, the elders in whom the jealously guarded treasure of ancestral experience lives on. Such a treasure is fragile and ever threatened with extinction because if he who knows it disappears, knowing will end. An individual discovery goes no further than the individual. Communal inheritance hangs on the continuity of men. It cannot be preserved and profited from outside the circle of the living. It must always be acting itself out and because of this fact its limits coincide with the capacities of human memory with all its distortions and fantasies.

Furthermore, one may well think that prehistoric man, precisely because he is ignorant of writing, does not know how to speak for himself. He only exists on the level of conversation, i.e. in participation. To this oral civilization there corresponds a diffuse culture, with an anonymous literature wherein the unsigned works belong to everyone and no one. It is the patriarchal age of the epic (etymologically: that which one expresses by speaking), of the legend (that which one relates), of the ballad, the tale, and the proverb. All these are popular treasures, the fruit of a collective unconscious. They are composed of words which fly and roam across the world, words all-too-often lost forever because, while they were still living, no one thought of fixing them once and for all.

The invention of writing overthrew the first human world and permitted the development of a new mental age. It is no exaggeration to say that it constitutes one of the essential factors in the disappearance of the mythical world of prehistory. Speech had given to man domination of his immediate space. But, bound to the concrete present, it can attain in scope and duration only an horizon limited to the fleeting boundaries of consciousness. Writing permits the separation of the voice from the present reality and thereby expands its range. Writings remain, and by that means they have the power to fix the world, to stabilize it in duration. Likewise, they crystallize and give form to a personality which then becomes capable of signing his name and of making himself felt beyond his bodily limits. Writing consolidates speech. It creates a deposit which can wait indefinitely for its reactivation in some consciousness to come. The historic personality poses before future generations. He inscribes on basalt, granite, or marble the chronicle of his deeds.

Thus the invention of writing frees man from the rule of tradition and hearsay. A new authority comes into being, that of the letter instead of custom. All of this takes place within a sacred environment. For the first writing is magical due to its miraculous powers. The first characters are hieroglyphics, that is to say divine signs, reserved for the priests and kings. Written statutes first appear on the law tablets, which the gods in heaven communicate to men. Divine code supercedes tradition and stabilizes the social order by making possible a civil administration of indefinite extent. The new authority is vested in a new type of man, men of writing, the literate priests and scribes who effectively practice their skill in jealously guarded secrecy. The very words of the gods become a sacred Scripture. The great religions, Judaism, Christianity, and Islam, thus rest upon the repository of a sacred text, the preservation and interpretation of which is assured by clergymen and commentators.

Reading and writing, then, are at first the monopoly of a privileged caste. The literate form an elite that is recognizable by the use of the written tongue, distinctly different from the spoken tongue. This is because "one never writes as one speaks," notes M. Vendryes; "one writes (or tries to write) as others write." [2] The vulgar tongue can never assume the dignity of writing. Even now, the pursuit of style is the distinctive sign of the written tongue, and the shortest letter forces us to resort to affected formulas which never occur in conversation. There exists in Mohammedan countries a literary Arabic that is a dead tongue maintained for writing purposes. Along side it there is a conversational Arabic that one speaks but doesn't write. This is why it has been said in our own time that a writer such as Valéry perpetuates in his books the written tongue of the 18th century which, since that time, has been distinguishable from the common tongue. And it is thus that the aristocratic character of writing is maintained, a character that imposes upon us an archaic and conventional authority—as if recourse to paper and pen activated in us another consciousness, distinct from speaking consciousness.

Writing, however, has ceased to be the privilege of the few. It plays the part of an essential minimum for

2. Vendryes, *Le Langage*, Renaissance du Livre, 121, p. 389.

contemporary man—at least this is true in the West, whereas the majority of the rest of humanity are still illiterate. A new technical revolution took place in the sixteenth century with the discovery of printing, a revolution that destroyed the conditions for spiritual existence by carrying the intellectual life from the craft age to that of industry. Henceforth, reading and writing are within the reach of all. The consumption of printed paper keeps on growing as the techniques of its utilization are perfected, so that today humanity continues to suffer from a latent crisis, a real scarcity of newsprint. From the sixteenth century on, the spread of books offers to each man, at the price of an initial education, the possibility of direct access to truth.

This event is of prime importance, for truth no longer favors any one person, caste, or class. The critical spirit is born. Each person is called to judge for himself what he ought to believe or think. The humanism of the Renaissance is founded on the publication of the Greek and Latin classics just as the Reformation is made possible by the wide distribution of the printed Bible. In a significant coincidence, the very same group of people who decide in 1536 to adopt the Reformation in Geneva likewise enact compulsory public education. That memorable development in the history of the West complements the demand of the new religious awareness seeking to provide each person access to the sacred texts. Moreover, at the same time and for the same reasons, modern literary tongues come into being. Until that time, Latin met the needs of the elite class of clergymen. For the increasingly important masses, writing and reading are no longer a matter of vocation, but an element of culture and the spiritual life. The intellectual development of these masses, then, fosters the formation of written languages based on merely spoken dialects.

Modern culture is a culture of the book. The printed word is so intimately associated with our lives that we have to some degree lost sight of its importance. But let us for a single day be deprived of a newspaper and we'll see just how right the Hegelian formula is that reading a newspaper is the morning prayer òf modern man. Printing gives us space and time, the world and others. The world in which our consciousness at each moment situates us is the expression of our reading and not the summary of our direct experience, so restricted in comparison. The role of speech keeps shrinking while the printed word endlessly increases the possibility of communication between men.

Besides, printing is not merely a technique for putting men in touch. It exerts its influence on the very structure of consciousness. The man who reads and writes is no longer the same as the one who owes his inclusion in humanity to speech alone. The values in play are profoundly modified. Speech is captive of a situation. It presupposes being face to face and is limited to a moment, a context of present emotion, which overloads it with enormous possibilities for understanding as well as for disagreement. In contrast, writing provides distance. It removes the reader from the enchantment of the present. It removes him from fleshly presence to a spiritual presence, from massive actuality filled with feeling to a more abstracted actuality, no longer based on the event but now based on thought. Even the most passionate pamphlet leaves the critical mind possibilities of intervention that an impassioned harangue completely destroys. In this respect, writing seems to be a reflection of speaking, a first abstraction tending to emphasize its true meaning. The written word is offered to us deprived of its living orchestration, at one and the same time both speech and silence. Absence and silence here are like a test that mellows decisions and confirms love. To be sure, there is no greater human achievement than the understanding of two human beings in authenticity, the full communion of two living persons. But beyond these exceptional moments, writing, which allows one's depths to speak and which gives echoes the time to come into being, offers immense possibilities to the spiritual life. It brings the dead back to life and allows our thought, in the privacy of leisure, to encounter the great spirits of all time. But still, if writing is to take on all its meaning, it is necessary for the reader to be able to receive this gift which is given to him. In the final reckoning, everything depends on his openness and his generosity.

Thus the discovery of printing was a veritable spiritual revolution for humanity. It seems that our own age, witnessing a proliferation of new techniques, is undergoing a no lesser convulsion, the consequences of which still escape us. The means of recording and transmitting speech are seeing an extraordinary growth. The telephone, telegraph, photography, phonograph, moving pictures, radio, and television play a role of ever-increasing importance in the existence of comtemporary man. These are no longer a matter of abstract writing. The voice is transmitted with all of its resonance and accompanies the very image of the person. And the image is faithfully represented in all of its detail, with its movement, its color, and sometimes even its relief. We see here a global restoration of reality. It's as if contemporary civilization, mass civilization which renders men absent from one another, were trying to compensate for that absence by increasing the possibilities of artificial presence. Contemporary man is familiar with the voice and image of all the great men of the earth. Moving pictures and newspaper illustrations give him a truly global awareness.

Undoubtedly, it is difficult to estimate the consequences of the so-rapid technical evolution we are witnessing and to predict in what way the men of the future will differ from us, used to considering commonplace inventions that seem semi-miraculous to us. Undoubtedly, it is wise to be on guard against either a too easy optimism or too profound a pessimism. It is as absurd to imagine that man himself will become better through the magic of the new instruments at his disposal as it is to become anxious lest the techniques of transmission uproot him from himself and stultify him forever. At best, one can but dream of what humanity will be like when learning how to read and write is no longer necessary, or when the widespread use of the taperecorder will allow speech to be directly recorded and then listened to without an intervening symbolization process. A roll of tape will replace the book and printing will become only a by-gone memory. Such a transformation will not simply revolutionize teaching. It will modify the very structure of thought—for thought does not exist outside of its instruments, as if pre-established before its embodiment. Just as speaking is not merely a means of expression, but a constitutive element of human reality, so too the techniques of mechanical recording will very probably make their influence felt at the level of personal affirmation itself in some unforeseeable way. The book culture will give way to an image and sound culture. Even now new arts are being born, and the human spirit can see opening before it exciting new vistas. Technology must deepen its own awareness, it must broaden man's self-awareness, and thereby add new provinces to human reality.

XII / Toward an Ethic of Speech

THE RESULT of our short study seems to be that only philosophy can provide an understanding of the total phenomenon of human speech. Numerous disciplines are bound up with this or that element of speech to the exclusion of the others. The activity of speaking is the object for psychobiological or phonetic investigations. The tongue as a social institution is the field of interest peculiar to linguistics, philology, and stylistics. And when we read this or that specialized study, we are often struck by its ingeniousness and its penetration. But somehow it seems to miss the basic point. Speech is not merely a tonal system, a neurological montage. Rather, it represents a constitutive element of human reality, so that the function of language only assumes its full meaning within the context of the total human experience. Likewise, it is only by abstraction that a tongue becomes a closed system, intelligible in itself. Lexicography, etymology, and even grammar only present us with intellectual mechanisms, disembodied and, so to speak, subordinate to that living reality the unity of which exists only in and through speaking subjects. The total phenomenon of speech is a personal phenomenon.

The result is that it escapes all positive determination. The spoken word can be presented as a substance, as a reality already there. But the essence of speech must be sought for in the act of speaking (*la parole parlante*—Merleau-Ponty), that is to say in the very activity in which speaking intervenes as productive reality, a vocation and an evocation of the world and man. This original act of speaking ultimately provides the only key to the intelligibility of the sensory-motor, phonetic, or linguistic phenomena. Specialists here cling to secondary causes. For example, they restore after the event the geneologies of sounds or words and the family relations of meanings. But they can only outline the changes of a history in which changes remain unpredictable. They decipher the how, whereas the why escapes them. The intellectual enjoyment so peculiar to linguistic studies results precisely from those unforeseen and picturesque ins and outs of the history of meanings. Words have a destiny that is happy or tragic according to the use men make of them. The "laws" of the various linguistic disciplines are limited in fact to describing certain aspects of historical development. They seek a reality which they can forever only approximate. In the human sciences, one can play the part of prophet only in the past. The future escapes the scientist because it puts into play a power of decision that no system of explanation has yet succeeded in making obey a material or intellectual norm.

The presence of freedom thus gives the human activity of speech its true dimension; it confirms the privileged position of metaphysics over physics. We have seen how speech assures the creation of the human world by the promotion of nature to culture. The initial transcendence of the Logos or the divine Word as it is manifested from the mythical point of view in all eschatologies is only the archetype of the effective operation imposed on every living man to constitute his vital space by the recovery of the linguistic elements immanent in the environment. The established language is only a possibility asking to be realized. Each man, whether conscious of it or not, is the master of his vocabulary as he is the master of his style. His manner of speaking is characteristic of his personal affirmation. In fact, speech intervenes as a principle of individuation.

In the final reckoning, then, the problem of speech seems to take all of its meaning from the moral order. Each man is responsible for constituting a universe for himself. That is to say, he is responsible for passing from the mental, moral, and even material confusion of infancy to the adult's presence to the world, a presence within the present moment articulated as a function of values which define his relations with the world and others. This is *the* adult task, a task which must be continually repeated because man is a historical being. The movement of time and the change of situation once again cast in doubt every balance once it is achieved. The very concern for continuity in truth obliges us to repeatedly create at each new moment. Thus speech defines any supreme moment of the person, the first or last word of his existence in its spontaneity, bearing witness to this unique being affirming and reaffirming himself over against the world.

This fundamental meaning of speech becomes evident in the sacred character that is generally conferred on it, beyond any religious reference. A kind of religion of speech exists even among those divorced from all religion properly speaking, as if a certain use of language could take the place of eschatology. Regulus keeps his word even at the cost of his life. The young officer of *Servitude and Military Grandeur,* a prisoner on his word of honor on board an English ship, sacrifices his career and his freedom to keep his word. A kind of unconditional moral imperative arises here, clothed in that sublimity which Kant saw in duty. To give one's word shows the human capacity of self-affirmation despite all material restrictions. It is the disclosure of a human being as he really is, the projection of value into existence. In a particularly tense situation in which my fate was at stake, I gave my word as the word appropriate to the situation, the word that resolved the situation and made me a new being in a world transformed. Others had confidence in me and I united myself to them by a commitment of mutual faith. To respect one's word is thus to respect others as well as oneself, for it indicates what one thinks of oneself. He who breaks his word is dishonored not only in the eyes of others, but in his own eyes as well.

The religion of speech is thus a criterion for personal authenticity. Giving one's word shows that human speech, not content merely to indicate value, can itself become a value. One's word of honor is a fixed point amidst all our vicissitudes: it is through the promise that we pass from personal time to personal eternity. It raises up life, a domain of habit and desire, to the rule of the norm, the consciousness of value by means of which the person makes up his mind to become what he is. Every word in this sense, even if it has not been pronounced as an oath, is a promise, and we ourselves must be careful not to desecrate a language which others read as the symbolic representation of our personal life.

Man, capable of speaking, thus finds himself clothed in a prophetic dignity. In the face of an uncertain future, speech formulates an anticipation. It traces within the chaos of circumstances the first hints of the future. In his own personal world, man acts with a power of creative initiative. The man who gives his word enunciates himself and announces himself, according to the direction he has taken, mobilizing all his resources to give birth to a reality fitting his demand. By the power of a word once pronounced, something begins to be which was not before. Speaking alters the form of the situation. It is a pledge and commitment, the signature of a contract which may appear to be a loss of freedom, but which in fact guarantees man's attainment of a new freedom through the power of obedience.

Thus speech at its most effective takes on the meaning of a *vow* or even a *sacrament*. It is speaking in action, a word that is a holy action, a moment of personal eschatology in which destiny is shaped. It is highly indicative of this sacramental value of speech that the Christian doctrine of marriage, all too often misunderstood, situates the sacrament in the mutual commitment of husband and wife. The priest is merely the first witness to a mutual assent whereby two lives are henceforth joined together. But it is also clear that if speech is promise, it is only valuable insofar as it is kept and in proportion to the capacity to keep it of whoever utters it. He has given a pledge. He remains master of the value that he himself attributes to this pledge. To keep one's word is to make an effort to maintain a certain sense of oneself that one once recognized as constituting his personal existence. Faithfulness, in marriage as in any other commitment, is not a routine, but corresponds to an inner repetition of the promise, a continual reactualization that makes of the word given an eternal present. It is not easy to keep speech as the only fixed point at the heart of a ceaselessly variable human reality, and perhaps any oath promises more than it is possible to hold to. But then the other danger arises of becoming slave to an out-of-date promise which time has made meaningless and which henceforth necessarily becomes a vain superstition. Man remains the master of his word, but he can only give up a dead fidelity in order to affirm a more living authenticity. In any case, the respect for commitments is self-respect, and everyone is judged in himself by his capacity for this essential loyalty.

Thus, it seems impossible in the abstract to fix rules for the correct use of speech. The task of the honest man cannot be assumed by anyone but himself. In any case, the cardinal virtues of fidelity, loyalty, and honor, and the vices of lying, hypocrisy, and perjury are bound up with the practice of language in good or bad faith. The man of his word is the one who, in a troubled world, strives to contribute to the realization of truth. Not that language by itself possesses a magical power. There are literally no more right words in this world than there are clean hands. Speech is worth no more than the man who uses it. The word appears in the flow of existence like a landmark or a guide—always both the beginning and the end. The spotless perfection of a definitive language, on the contrary, would bring language to a full stop and would ruin existence by stabilizing it.

The ethic of speech indicates a need for veracity as a daily experience. It's a question of telling the truth, but there is no telling the truth without being true. And so the necessity of clearing up the relations of self to others and self to self becomes definite. Here, the commandments are clear. First of all will be the refusal to pay lip-service, to pay oneself and others with words that are not, as they should be, so many pledges of the inner self. Let speaking be whole and always indicative of a real presence. Verbal facility all too often hides character flaw. The man of his word doesn't just give lip-service, but gives himself. And that purification of speech is double-edged, it implies a reciprocal clause. One must let others speak, being on guard against behaving like those who take over the whole conversation for themselves and never listen to what one says to them. To be open to the speech of others is to grasp it in its best sense, continually striving not to reduce it to the common denominator of banality, but to find in it something original. By doing this, moreover, by helping the other to use his own voice, one will stimulate him to discover his innermost need. Such is the task of the teacher, if, going beyond the monologue of instruction, he knows how to carry the pedagogical task into authentic dialogue where personality is developed. The great educator is he who spreads around himself the meaning of the honor of language as a concern for integrity in the relations with others and oneself.

The man of his word affirms himself at the heart of an ambiguous human reality as a guide and landmark, as an element of calm certainty. Doubtlessly, he runs the risk of loneliness and failure. One cannot be true all alone, nor play the game alone if all the others cheat. Such at least is the easy excuse of those who try to justify breaking their word by pointing to the laxity of others. Certainly if everyone spoke the truth, it would be easy to do likewise. But the moral task consists in taking the initiative in the direction of obedience to value rather than custom. One must be true without waiting for others to be so, and precisely so that others might come to be so. The strong personality engenders an environment of truth around itself. Its strictness is contagious and it carries others along with its momentum. The man of truth radiates a kind of light that forces each witness to see and judge himself. A Socrates, a Jesus, or a Gandhi imposes on his listeners that authority which he is the first to obey. His speaking exercises an intrinsic efficacy that makes others consent.

The man of his word, pursuing for his own good the goal of being true, thereby contributes to putting human reality in order. He knows perfectly well that he will never finish his work, but he has a faith in the possibility of a better understanding between men, of a more authentic communication. Our duty is for each of us to take on the creative initiative which is the function of the Word. A man's life must achieve on its own the elevation of nature to culture, animality to humanity. Of course, this emergence is facilitated by society itself, which takes charge of the child and fashions him according to the norms of his environment. But this environmental education is never completely sufficient. The passage from chaos to cosmos must be ceaselessly repeated. The upward struggle must constantly win out over the threats of coasting downhill. Speech fixes the determination of man, who, by means of the promise and the vow, proves to himself and others that he is the master of his temporal existence. But, while and by forming himself, the man of his word also works toward human unity. The cultural background of humanity is composed of promises begun, promises given, promises kept, and promises broken. It is true, as the wisdom of China has declared, that the order and harmony of the world rest upon unity in language. Now our age offers the spectacle of a dislocated humanity, a humanity divided against itself and prey to the curse of Babel. We live the confusion of tongues and face the impossibility of friendship because men, when all is said and done, no longer understand one another. Above all, that which is lacking in our age is the community of values which alone might found the language of a single culture, within each country as well as between nations. Undoubtedly, no single person can presume to discover by himself the solution that would enable the world to be extricated from the mire of misunderstanding. But every man participates in the human endeavor, and each man must be concerned with saving it from its curse. Each man can contribute to creating a better world, a world prepared, announced, and even brought into being by every word that is a harbinger of good faith and authenticity. Each man may see to it that words take on value wherever he is, that is that confidence and peace reign in the commonwealth. The meaning of every fate may be written along the sad and yet triumphant road from Babel to the Pentecost. But the moral person can still undertake the task of accomplishing in the world his supreme function so that one day he can say about himself those words which the wise emperor of China had engraved on his statue: "I have brought order to the mass of human beings and put deeds and realities to the test: each thing has the name which suits it."

Bibliography

For the reader who wishes to pursue some of the reflections introduced in this book, the following selected bibliography is offered.

Carroll, J. B.: *The Study of Language*, Harvard University Press, Cambridge, 1953

Cassirer, Ernst: *The Philosophy of Symbolic Forms*, Vol. 1, Yale University Press, New Haven, 1953

Dufrenne, Mikel: *Language and Philosophy*, Indiana University Press, Bloomington, 1963

Gendlin, Eugene T.: *Experiencing and the Creation of Meaning*, Free Press of Glencoe, New York, 1962

Goldstein, Kurt: *Language and Language Disturbances*, Grune and Stratton, New York, 1948

Heidegger, Martin: *Unterwegs zur Sprache*, Neske, Pfullingen, 1959

Heveni, J. L. (ed.): *Essays on Language and Literature*, Allen Wingate, London,

Kaelin, Eugene F.: *An Existentialist Aesthetic*, University of Wisconsin Press, Madison, 1962

Merleau-Ponty, Maurice: *Phenomenology of Perception*, Humanities Press, New York, 1962

Merleau-Ponty, Maurice: *The Primacy of Perception and Other Essays*, Northwestern University Press, Evanston, 1964

Merleau-Ponty, Maurice: *Signs*, Northwestern University Press, Evanston, 1964

Mohanty, J. N.: *Edmund Husserl's Theory of Meaning*, Nijhoff, The Hague, 1964

Parain, Brice: *Recherches sur la Nature et les Fonctions du Langage*, Paris, 1942

Pos, H. J.: "Phénoménologie et Linguistique," *Revue Internationale de Philosophies*, Paris, 1939

Saussure, Ferdinand de: *Course in General Linguistics*, Philosophical Library, New York, 1959

Snell, Bruno: *Der Aufbau der Sprache*, Classen, Hamburg, 1952

Strauss, Erwin: *The Primary World of the Senses*, Free Press of Glencoe, New York, 1963

Index of Names

Alain, 53, 82
Alcibiades, 76
Amiel, 53
Aristotle, 20, 21, 28, 102
Augustine, St., 96

Balzac, 88
Baudelaire, 83
Beethoven, 94
Bergson, 38, 52, 53
Berkeley, 30, 102
Blondel, 53
Brunschvicg, 53
Brutus, 41
Buffon, 75
Byrd, 100

Che Houang-ti, 14
Claudel, 89
Comte, 52
Condillac, 30, 31
Confucius, 14

Debussy, 89
Delacroix, 37, 49
Descartes, 26, 27, 28, 29, 30,
    31, 55, 102
de Sévigné, 106
Diderot, 3, 106
Dostoevsky, 88

Dujardin, 99
Durkheim, 52, 53

Einstein, 38
Eugenio d'Ors, 101

Faulkner, 99
Fénelon, 109

Galileo, 25, 29
Gandhi, 126
Gide, 70, 106
Goethe, 73
Gracian, 105

Hamlet, 41
Humboldt, 31

Jaspers, 81, 91
Jesus, 126
Joyce, 99

Kant, 38, 102, 122
Kepler, 26, 29
Kierkegaard, 79, 81

La Bruyére, 106
Leibniz, 28, 102
Lenéru, 94
Locke, 30

Maine de Biran, 53
Mairan, 102
Malebranche, 102
Mallarmé, 51, 74, 83, 89, 106
Marchioness of Rambouillet,
    105
Maurice de Guérin, 106
Mersenne, 26, 28, 30
Monet, 89
Montaigne, 53, 55, 94
Montesquieu, 106
Moses, 16

Newton, 26, 38
Nietzsche, 38

Ovid, 64

Parain, 43
Pascal, 105
Peter, St., 16
Piaget, 13
Plato, 20, 21, 22, 25, 28
Plotinus, 78
Proust, 55

Racine, 106
Renan, 31
Renard, 106
Richelieu, 15, 62
Rilke, 82
Rimbaud, 83
Rousseau, 106

Sainte-Beuve, 73
Sartre, 38
Sebatier, 105
Socrates, 20, 21, 41, 82, 102,
    126
Spinoza, 26
Stirner, 55

Tolstoi, 106

Valéry, 83, 112
Vendryes, 60, 112
Vigny 55, 106
Voltaire, 106
Von Hofmannstahl, 65

Wagner, 67